the **About.com** guide to

WEB
DESIGN

**Build and Maintain a Dynamic, User-Friendly Web Site
Using HTML, CSS, and JavaScript**

Jennifer Kyrnin
The About.com Guide to Web Design/HTML

Aadamsmedia
Avon, Massachusetts

About **About.com**

About.com is a powerful network of more than 600 Guides—smart, passionate, accomplished people who are experts in their fields. About.com Guides live and work in more than twenty countries and celebrate their interests in thousands of topics. They have written books, appeared on national television programs, and won many awards in their fields. Guides are selected for their ability to provide the most interesting information for users and for their passion for their subject and the Web. The selection process is rigorous—only 2 percent of those who apply actually become Guides. The following are the most important criteria by which they are chosen:

- High level of knowledge and passion for their topic
- Appropriate credentials
- Keen understanding of the Web experience
- Commitment to creating informative, inspiring features

Each month more than 48 million people visit About.com. Whether you need home-repair and decorating ideas, recipes, movie trailers, or car-buying tips, About.com Guides offer practical advice and solutions for everyday life. If you're looking for how-to advice on refinishing your deck, for instance, About.com shows you the tools you need to get the job done. No matter where you are on About.com or how you got there, you'll always find exactly what you're looking for!

About Your Guide

 Jennifer Kyrnin has been a professional Web developer, designer, and Web site manager for over 12 years. She has worked on small personal sites as well as huge corporate sites. Jennifer started at About.com in 1997, as the About.com Guide to HTML. Her site was then updated to cover HTML and XML, and in 2000 she took over the Web Design site and began running the About.com Web Design/HTML site. Her Web site covers everything a Web developer needs to plan, build, and maintain a Web site.

Building Web sites and helping others build Web sites has been a passion for Jennifer almost since the birth of the World Wide Web. Jennifer worked at NETCOM On-Line Communications in the early 1990s, and there she helped create one of the first Web-based technical support knowledge bases. When she joined the Web team as a Web writer, she was hired to write the content and HTML while her team members built programs to support the site. From there she went on to build some marketing Web sites for small businesses and then moved on to Symantec, where she helped build and maintain the Symantec Web site for nearly nine years.

Jennifer loves the Web and the Internet and wants to make it fun for anyone who wants to build a Web page.

Acknowledgments

I would like to thank Betsy for helping me come up with ideas even when she didn't know she was doing it—it helped to talk horses when I should have been writing. Thanks to my parents and brother for their support, and to Shasta and McKinley for inspiration when I was sure I wouldn't be able to build a Web page about anything. And thanks to Mark for everything. I couldn't have done it without you!

ABOUT.COM

CEO & President
Scott Meyer

COO
Andrew Pancer

SVP Content
Michael Daecher

Director, About Operations
Chris Murphy

Marketing Communications Manager
Lisa Langsdorf

ADAMS MEDIA

Editorial

Innovation Director
Paula Munier

Editorial Director
Laura M. Daly

Executive Editor
Brielle K. Matson

Development Editor
Katie McDonough

Marketing

Director of Marketing
Karen Cooper

Assistant Art Director
Frank Rivera

Production

Director of Manufacturing
Susan Beale

Production Project Manager
Michelle Roy Kelly

Senior Book Designer
Colleen Cunningham

About.com® is a registered trademark of About, Inc.

Published by Adams Media, an F+W Publications Company
57 Littlefield Street
Avon, MA 02322
www.adamsmedia.com

ISBN-10: 1-59869-378-6
ISBN-13: 978-1-59869-378-2

Printed in China.

J I H G F E D C B A

Library of Congress Cataloging-in-Publication Data
is available from the publisher.

This publication is designed to provide accurate and authoritative information with regard to the subject matter covered. It is sold with the understanding that the publisher is not engaged in rendering legal, accounting, or other professional advice. If legal advice or other expert assistance is required, the services of a competent professional person should be sought.

—From a *Declaration of Principles* jointly adopted by a Committee of the American Bar Association and a Committee of Publishers and Associations

Many of the designations used by manufacturers and sellers to distinguish their product are claimed as trademarks. Where those designations appear in this book and Adams Media was aware of a trademark claim, the designations have been printed with initial capital letters.

This book is available at quantity discounts for bulk purchases. For information, please call 1-800-289-0963.

How to Use This Book

Each About.com book is written by an About.com Guide—a specialist with expert knowledge of his or her subject. Although the book can stand on its own as a helpful resource, it may also be coupled with its corresponding About.com site for further tips, tools, and advice. Each book not only refers you back to About.com but also directs you to other useful Internet locations and print resources.

All About.com books include a special section at the end of each chapter called Get Linked. There you'll find a few links back to the About.com site for even more useful information on the topics discussed in that chapter. Depending on the topic, you will find links to such resources as photos, sheet music, quizzes, recipes, or product reviews.

About.com books also include four types of sidebars:

- **Ask Your Guide:** Detailed information in a question-and-answer format
- **Tools You Need:** Advice about researching, purchasing, and using a variety of tools for your projects
- **What's Hot:** All you need to know about the hottest trends and tips out there
- **Elsewhere on the Web:** References to other useful Internet locations

Each About.com book takes you on a personal tour of a certain topic, gives you reliable advice, and leaves you with the knowledge you need to achieve your goals.

CONTENTS

CONTENTS . . . *continued*

Introduction from Your Guide

Web design and HTML have come a long way since I started building Web sites in 1995. Back then it was big news to be able to put images on a page. We were desperate to get our customers off of the Lynx browser so that they'd see the images we'd labored so long on.

Those were the days of rainbow-colored horizontal rules, pages where everything was centered, the background was black and the text was red or something equally unreadable, and if you could get a horrible-sounding WAV file to play when the page loaded, everyone knew that you were a hot Web developer. The images took forever to download and most of the time they were animated. And Ajax was still called DHTML or JavaScript and didn't work very well when it was on a site.

A lot has changed. Corporations have entered the World Wide Web with a vengeance; everyday people run blogs and send out podcasts; and watching a video on YouTube is something you do all the time, not just from the fast connection at work.

But a lot has also stayed the same. Sites with black backgrounds and red or equally unreadable font colors abound on the Web. And while we might not hear as many horrible-sounding WAV files, lots of sites still have images so large they take forever to download, even on a DSL or cable line.

It doesn't have to be that way. The Web is an exciting place to do business, and it's something that every business, large or small, should be interested in getting into. I want this book to be a place for you to learn how to create a Web site for your business and for pleasure.

Web sites are easy to make, and it can be a lot of fun building Web sites that have color and style and pizzazz. This isn't a step-by-step book on how to learn HTML or CSS. There are lots of great books and Web sites on that; I even have classes on my Web site where you can learn both of those languages. What I will do is take you through the steps to imagine, plan, build, and maintain a Web site. You'll use standards-based techniques so your site will stand the test of time. And you'll get clued in to lots of other resources so that you can continue your learning.

Once you start building Web pages, chances are you won't want to stop. And this book and the About.com Web Design/ HTML site are designed to start you on the path to building exciting Web sites with modern designs.

I love to build Web pages, and I love to help other people build Web pages. I have set up a special area of my Web Design/ HTML Web site for this book (**http://about.com/webdesign/book**). All of the links found here can also be found on my Web site by chapter. You'll also be able to see the examples from the chapters and sample code. And if you have any questions about this book or building a Web page, feel free to e-mail me at *webdesign .guide@about.com*. I'd love to hear from you!

Chapter 1

The Big Picture

Getting Started Building a Web Site

Whether you're looking to build a **Web site** for your business or you just want to create a personal blog or photo site, you're in for an exciting experience. These days most businesses have Web sites; it's a great way to get your product out there and show the world what services you offer. More and more people are also using Web sites to keep in touch with friends and family, to meet new people, and to showcase art, music, and more.

If you've never created a Web site, you're probably a little nervous. Luckily, building a Web site is only as challenging as you want it to be. Many successful Web sites use only a small number of **HTML tags** and still look nice and serve the needs of their customers.

You may be surprised at how quickly you can have a Web site up and running. I have had students build a working Web site in one or two days. By the time you're finished this book, you will understand the HTML basics needed to build a Web site, and you'll have all the tools you need to meet your goals.

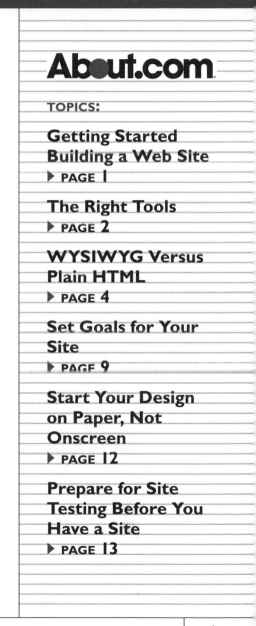

There are a few things that you need to get started: good software, a great plan, and a winning attitude. Attitude is the most important. If you have a positive outlook, then your Web site will turn out fine and you'll have what you need to make it even better.

The best advice I can give you right now is to start simple. You can always make your site more complicated later. Starting with grand ideas and a simple plan is better than starting with a grand plan and not knowing how to implement it. Remember that you can always add more to your site, but trying to do it all right away will result in a Web site that's only half finished.

The Right Tools

With all jobs, the importance of the right tools cannot be overstated. In designing a Web site, there are tools you need and tools that are nice to have. It can be easy to get hung up on the bells and whistles of different tools and applications, but do you need **Flash** when you haven't even got a Web site up? And is it vital that you buy an image **roll-over** builder? What if you decide you don't want to use image roll-overs?

Choosing a good HTML editor is important. Other than the computer itself, your editor is the tool you will use the most. HTML editors can be fancy or bare bones; they can help you build your graphics or show you when your HTML is correct. Some of the most popular Web editors are the following:

- **Dreamweaver:** This is the most popular HTML editor, but it's also one of the more expensive. It's available for both Windows and Macintosh.
- **FrontPage:** Microsoft's WYSIWYG editor is available only for Windows, but if you're comfortable with the Word interface, you might like this HTML editor.

- **BBEdit:** Many Macintosh users use BBEdit to build Web pages, but it's not a WYSIWYG editor.
- **Notepad:** This is not an HTML editor, but it comes free with the Windows **operating system** (**OS**), so many people prefer to use it. I don't recommend using Notepad, as it can cause more problems than it solves. But if you must, be sure to read my article on editing Web pages with Notepad (http://about.com/webdesign/htmlinnotepad).
- **nVu:** A WYSIWYG editor that is free under the GNU software license. This editor works in Windows, Macintosh, and Linux or Unix operating systems.

Don't focus only on price when deciding what HTML editor to use. Many other features can make a difference when building Web pages. Yes, several hundred dollars may seem like a lot to shell out for a Web design tool, but in the long run, you'll more than cover the cost if it's what you need.

First you need to evaluate your needs. Choose a Web design editor that will help you build and maintain your site for a long time. While your site may be fairly simple right now, it's important to remember that it will get bigger in the future. Ask yourself these questions:

- What operating system do you use for your day-to-day work? (It doesn't matter what the **server** OS is.)
- Do you want to learn HTML or do you want a visual WYSIWYG editor?
- Do you need an integrated graphics program?
- Will you be using more advanced technologies now or in the future like **PHP, ASP, XML**, or databases?
- Will your site be translated into other languages?
- How much are you willing to pay for an HTML editor?

WHAT'S HOT

▶ Wondering whether to go with WYSIWYG (which stands for what you see is what you get), HTML editors, or text editors? This is a question that's on the mind of many Web designers. In my poll (http://about.com/webdesign/editorpoll), I've found people who feel very strongly about the issue. Some hate WYSIWYG editors while others never use text editors. But don't let the arguments scare you. If WYSIWYG works better for you then that's what you should use. I use both types of editor all the time.

Your operating system is where you'll be doing all your work. Many Web designers prefer the Macintosh operating system, and there are many HTML editors available for both Macintosh and Windows. I have not found that it makes a difference which OS you use, as most of the better Web-design editors are available for both Windows and the Mac as well as Unix/Linux.

It doesn't matter what OS your Web server is running. Even if you are on a Mac at home and your server is Windows, you shouldn't have any problems connecting to your server and putting up your Web pages. This may be an issue if you were to edit your files right on the Web server, but this is a dangerous habit to get into, and I don't recommend it.

WYSIWYG Versus Plain HTML

In this book, you will learn basic HTML, so I recommend getting an editor that has both HTML editing capabilities and WYSIWYG, even if you aren't yet comfortable with HTML.

WYSIWYG is actually something of a misnomer, as it's very difficult to know what you're going to "get" on a Web page. Everyone who visits your Web page will be using different software on different operating systems with different settings, and all these can change how your Web page will look. If you're using a WYSIWYG editor, you can be lulled into a sense of complacency. Your Web page might look nice in your editor but bad in some Web browsers. I have seen this happen even with the most popular editor, Dreamweaver. Another problem that some WYSIWYG editors have is generating bad HTML code. Your pages look okay, but the HTML that creates them is bloated and causes your pages to download more slowly. In extreme cases the page won't load correctly or at all in some Web browsers.

HTML isn't that hard to learn. If you must have a WYSIWYG editor, a lot come with code editors included. The best way to become comfortable building Web pages in HTML is to build them using a code editor without WYSIWYG functionality. You can always test your pages and make sure they're looking correct as you build them. It can be a little slower when you're first learning, but you'll have fewer problems later than you would if you relied solely on a WYSIWYG editor.

Integrated graphics editing increases the price. Many of the lesser-known editors that offer integrated graphics editing do not offer the same flexibility as a separate graphics program.

I have found that it's better to stick with an HTML editor that just does HTML and leave the graphics editing to another program. If your site won't have a lot of graphics, you might not need an expensive graphics editor. I'll cover graphics editors in greater detail later in this chapter.

Always plan to use advanced technology. Right now your site may only have simple images and text. But if it takes off, you may want to integrate a **blogging tool** or a database. If your editor can't easily handle languages other than HTML, you'll spend additional money on one that does. Having a Web editor that supports other technology is a good idea.

People usually forget internationalization. It's easy to forget, but if your company goes global, being able to edit Web sites in other languages can be crucial.

If your Web page editor can't handle special characters like "á," then you won't be able to translate your site into Latin-1 languages like Spanish or French, even if the translation is provided by someone else. I have posted pages in Spanish, French, Portuguese,

WHAT'S HOT

▶ I offer a free ten-week HTML course on my About .com site: http://about.com/ webdesign/htmlcourse. If ten weeks seems like a long time, you can always request the classes more quickly, or you can run through the online tutorial version of the class on your own (http://about. com/webdesign/htmltutorial).

Russian, Italian, Korean, and simplified Chinese as well as other languages. I don't speak or read most of those languages, but since my Web editor can handle the codes, I don't need to.

Lastly, decide how much you want to pay. Price should not be your first or only criterion, but unless you're independently wealthy it will be a factor. Luckily, there are many choices in Web-design editors at various price levels—from free to several hundred dollars and lots in between. Also, just because the software costs money doesn't make it good. One of my least favorite editors costs around $40, while one of my favorite Windows WYSIWYG editors is free.

What do I recommend? I prefer HomeSite. This is a text HTML editor that comes with Dreamweaver. I have been using HomeSite for nine years, so I am very familiar with it. I like Home-Site because it gives me access to the HTML directly, without a lot of extra bells and whistles.

However, Dreamweaver is the software I usually recommend to new clients. It is a WYSIWYG program, but it allows you to edit the HTML directly. When I use Dreamweaver, I use it in split view so that I can write the code and see what it's doing to the design directly.

Figure 1-1: Dreamweaver in split-view mode

You don't have to buy Dreamweaver to get HomeSite. Adobe offers it for sale on their Web site and even offers a free thirty-day trial (**www.adobe.com/products/homesite**). If you decide to use HomeSite, you will learn a lot more about HTML more quickly than if you use a different tool.

Graphics editors can be important, too. If your site is going to have a lot of original graphics (rather than unedited **stock photography** or **clip art**, you'll need a graphics editor (**http://about.com/graphicssoft/graphicseditor**). I prefer Adobe Photoshop, but many people swear by Corel's Paint Shop Pro. I've got an article about choosing a graphics software tool geared toward Web designers on my site (**http://about.com/webdesign/graphicstools**).

But even if you use stock photography or clip art you may need a graphics editor. When you use images on your Web site, you can resize them using a graphics editor or ask the Web browser viewing the page to resize the image. The problem with having the Web browser resize the images is that they take the same time to download as if they were full size. Also, browsers usually resize the image badly so they don't look good on your Web pages.

For example, if you want to take photographs of your products for your product pages, your digital camera will take photos that are at least 640 × 480 **pixels** and between 18 and 32KB or more in size (extremely small for modern digital cameras). But on Web pages, smaller is better. Product images should be no more than 200 to 300 pixels square and only 5 to 10KB. If you have the Web browser resize the image, it must download the large 18KB image and then compress it to the size you specify. But Web browsers aren't graphics editors. Because Web browsers don't know how to resize images so that they still look nice, your customers see a jagged and ugly graphic. Chapter 12 covers more about editing images.

Unless you plan to hire someone to manage and maintain your images for you, it's a good idea to get a good Web graphics editor. Next to your HTML editor, a graphics editor is the second most important tool you should buy.

Get your Web pages on the Web with FTP. Many Web editors have **FTP** built right into the software. If your Web editor does not, you'll need to get an FTP client to move your Web files from your hard drive to your Web site.

I use FTP Voyager or Putty, because of its secure FTP functionality, to access sites that don't allow standard FTP connections. Putty is a free **telnet/ssh** client, but you can download a version with secure FTP. Find out more about FTP programs on my About .com site (**http://about.com/webdesign/ftpprograms**).

But that's not all the software you might need. Web designers use lots of tools to build a Web site, including these:

- **Web browsers:** Most Web designers have a lot of browsers. On my Windows machine I have Firefox, Internet Explorer (IE), Mozilla, Netscape, and Opera. On my Mac I have Firefox, Internet Explorer, Netscape, and Safari. With editors like Netscape I have multiple versions. Unfortunately, IE doesn't allow you to install multiple versions on one computer.
- **Validators:** Link checkers, HTML validators, and **CSS** validators all check your code to make sure it is correct. I use the validator included in HomeSite, but I also use the online validator at the W3C (**http://validator.w3.org**) to check my pages against standards.
- **Log analyzers:** Once your site starts getting a lot of page views, you'll want to review them with a tool so that you can keep improving your site. I currently use a home-built

log-analysis tool to review site statistics, but Google Analytics is a free application that is gaining a lot of popularity. Web-Trends is one of the more popular offline tools available.

- **Flash:** If you want more advanced applications on your site, Flash is a great tool, but it's very complex and difficult to learn. Flash refers to both the software and the resulting application on your site. The most common software used to create Flash files is Adobe Flash, but you can also use other programs to create Flash applications.
- **XML editors:** XML is another technology that can help you improve your Web site through database connectivity and other things. My favorite tool for editing XML is XMLSpy. This is available as a licensed version for Web teams.

Set Goals for Your Site

It's amazing how many people building a Web site simply sit down at their computer, open up the HTML editor, and start banging away. This might work fine for a personal Web site, but for a business Web site planning is crucial. A plan for your site will ensure that you are covering everything your business needs, and it will set up logical site areas that make it easier for your customers to find what they need.

There are several things to think about when sitting down to plan your Web site:

- What do you want your site to do?
- What will your customers want from the site?
- How will people move around your Web site?
- What type of content will you want on the site?

The first thing to figure out when planning a Web site is what you want it to accomplish. Some people refer to this

ELSEWHERE ON THE WEB

▶ One of my favorite but less well-known Web design software vendors is CoffeeCup (www.coffeecup.com), offering nearly every type of tool to build a Web site. For example, there is a HTML editor, a graphics resizer, a Webcam, a style sheet maker, and much more. Most are available with a trial download, and some are even offered for free.

as the business needs of the Web site. If you know what your Web site needs to do to be successful, you can measure against that goal and better ensure your success. For example, you might want to sell products or services online, to provide information about a topic, or a combination of both.

My site at About.com has the goal of providing my readers accurate and up-to-date information about Web Design, HTML, and XML. I know that from my initial plan of the site, and whenever I add new features, I can keep that focus in mind.

I've also built sites with more of a product focus. These sites have the goal of selling products or services. The owners of a product site might want the site to drive customers to the products or information about the products so they can buy them in a store. Whenever new features are added to these sites, they have the purpose of driving customers to the items for sale.

Your goal for your Web site might be a combination of both products and content. Most Web sites are a combination of both. For example, I do book reviews on my About.com site, and I would love it if people bought the books that they found there. But this is secondary to providing content. Always be aware of the primary goal of your site, and do not let secondary goals overpower the site.

What do your customers want? It would be nice if customers wanted the same things from a Web site that the designers do, but this isn't the case. For example, you might be planning to build a site to sell homemade pet toys. Your goal for the site is to advertise your pet toys and get people to buy them. Most Web customers don't have the goal of buying anything. They come to your site looking for pet toy information or for suggestions of toys that Dachshunds might like. If you don't meet the goals of your customers, they won't help you meet your goals.

The site structure, or the way the site is presented, is essential for your Web site. Structure is not the look of the site but rather how the information flows around the site. This is called information architecture. Planning your site structure is very important, as it gives you the framework to hang your designs and content on. You'll read more about site structure in Chapter 2.

Site structure helps your customers get around your Web site and find what they need to meet their goals so that you can meet your goals. This is so important that I dedicated all of Chapter 2 to the concept.

Finally, plan the site content. Some of it will be obvious. If you are building a product-focused site, you'll need product pages, and if you're building a content-focused site, you'll need content pages.

Right now you may not have many articles to promote or products to sell, but eventually you will. It's impossible to know everything you'll want in the future, but if there are things that you think would be interesting eventually, then plan for them in your Web design.

For example, you eventually might want to have the following features on your Web site:

TOOLS YOU NEED

▶ If you're interested in seeing the books I've reviewed, you can find them online at http://about.com/webdesign/bookreviews. I also review Web design software on the site at http://about.com/webdesign/softwarereviews. There you'll find reviews on HTML editors, browsers, FTP clients, and other related software.

- A **Weblog** (or several) where you can talk about your products
- **Podcast** articles about your topic for people to listen to
- Flash movies or games
- Links to other Web sites
- A database of products, services, or articles
- Online technical or customer support
- A forum, chat room, or other community portal

Most of these elements are beyond the scope of new Web sites, but they aren't unreasonable to build eventually. If you haven't

▶ It used to be that the Web designer did everything on a Web site, but now there are a lot of new fields opening up—from usability expert to user experience manager to information architect. In my ongoing poll on Web design titles (http://about.com/webdesign/titlespoll), information architect is starting to be more and more popular—and more specific than Web designer. Who knows what the job titles will be next year.

planned for them, it will be hard to add them. Or if you add them, they will be hard for customers to find.

The key to this is flexibility. While you may not know what new elements you'll need on your Web site, if you've got a design that can flex to meet your needs it won't matter. For example, all new articles on my About.com site are placed in categories. But if I write an article that doesn't fit into an existing category, I can always create a new category. The structure was set up so that I don't have to decide ahead of time the exact topics I'll cover. When **Ajax** became popular on Web sites, I didn't worry that I didn't have an Ajax area because my site design was flexible enough that I could add one.

Start Your Design on Paper, Not Onscreen

I've found that it's easier to think about a Web site if you start planning it away from the computer. When you're sitting at the computer, it's tempting to start building the Web pages, which defeats the purpose of planning in advance. If you start on paper, you'll be less inclined to worry about how the pages should look and focus more on what you're planning. But what should you be planning?

Determine where your Web site will be hosted and what software will be used to host your site. The biggest consideration regarding back-end software is the operating system of your Web host. The three choices for Web hosts are Unix or Linux (called *nix for short), Windows, and Macintosh.

For your initial plan, decide which operating system (OS) to use for your server. The most common OS for Web servers is Linux. There are advantages to each OS, and in Chapter 3, I cover how to choose a hosting provider.

Prepare for Site Testing Before You Have a Site

If you start testing your site before it's built, you can avoid problems before a lot of work has been done. Here are some points to keep in mind:

- You might be surprised at what people want from your site. Your customers may want something completely different from what you were preparing to build.
- Even the words you use in planning can affect how your site will turn out. If you start testing terms early, you might find ones that resonate with your audience.
- Customers can provide great ideas. Testing will give you new ideas you may never have thought of.

When you are starting out with your idea for a Web site, plan on doing usability testing in focus groups and market testing. If you've got a company set up to help you do testing right from the start, your site will be that much more effective.

It is possible to start your usability testing on your own. If all you have is a print-out of your Web page concept, you can take that around to your friends and have them critique it. An even better test would be to try to find some potential customers and ask them what they think of your idea.

Testing is key to building a Web site. But you have to keep an open mind. If you're willing to listen to what your friends and potential customers say about your ideas, you'll have a better site right from the start.

ELSEWHERE ON THE WEB

▶ Usability testing is best done by professionals in the field, and luckily the Web has been around long enough that many companies specialize in it. The U.S. Department of Health and Human Services provides a site specifically for creating usable Web sites (www.usability.gov). Jakob Nielsen, a premier Web usability expert, offers articles and information on Web usability on his site (www.useit.com).

Get Linked

Starting a Web site can be daunting, but it's absolutely possible to successfully create a site that works for you. The following links to my About.com site will help you get started.

HTML EDITORS

Choosing your editor is the most important task you can do when starting out building a Web site. The links on this page cover many of the most popular HTML editors and give tips and tricks for choosing and using them.

http://about.com/webdesign/htmleditors

TEN TIPS TO A GREAT WEB PAGE

Building a Web page is more than knowing HTML and good design. These tips are useful to keep in mind as you're planning your site and as you build and maintain it.

http://about.com/webdesign/webpagetips

IF YOU BUILD IT, WILL THEY COME?

Understanding your audience is vital to creating a Web site, and this article will help you create a site that people want to visit.

http://about.com/webdesign/sitepromotion

Chapter 2

Building a Site Structure

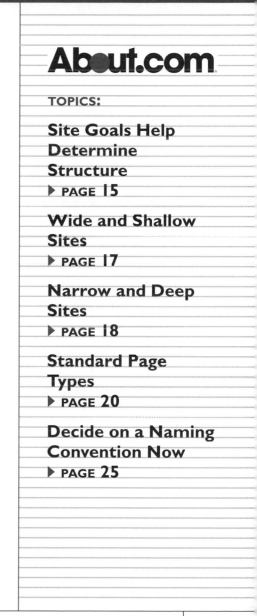

Site Goals Help Determine Structure

In Chapter 1, you determined the goals for your Web site. These goals will help you establish the best site structure so your customers can find what they need. There are two structures you can choose from: narrow and deep, or wide and shallow. These structures are well suited to the two types of sites we discussed in Chapter 1: product- and content-focused sites.

Content-focused sites have many things in common. The first is the goal of delivering informative content to their customers. These sites make money by selling access to the content or from advertisements on the pages with the content. So the goal of the site is to get the customer to the content she wants as quickly as possible. A typical secondary goal is to keep the customer moving through the site reading and reviewing additional content.

Content-focused sites are narrow and deep in structure because they want the customers to find the topic of interest and then delve deeply into it. These sites usually have an obvious categorization structure defined on the home page that helps their customers delve down into the site.

Product-focused sites are focused on selling products. They want to get people to the products for sale as quickly as possible. These sites make money by selling the product so there is less emphasis on getting customers to information and more on showcasing products and providing reasons to buy.

Product-focused sites are typically wide and shallow in structure. Unless there are a huge number of products available for sale, it's better to get as many of the products as possible in front of the customers. The home page of a product-focused site might have more links on it than a content-focused site, but there won't be a lot of subsections on the inner pages.

The most challenging is a mixed-focus site. Before you move forward, do some user testing. You will have more success if you focus on one type rather than trying to do both. Find out what your customers want and deliver that.

Once you know what your customers want, refine your goals. It's okay to have a mixed-focus site, but know which type of site your customers (or your business) will best support. Tailor your Web site design to match the focus, but allow room for your secondary focus.

For example, my husband runs the About.com PC Hardware Web site (http://compreviews.about.com), which is primarily a product site. He provides reviews of computer hardware and systems and wants his customers to see all the different products at once. But he also provides information, such as how to install motherboards or build a new computer. His primary focus is on products and is wider and shallower than a purely information site. Contrast

▶ The best site is a site where what you want your customers to do is also what they want to do. Creating a site that makes people want to buy seems obvious, but it's amazing how few people remember to do it. I examined several popular e-commerce sites and evaluated how they were so successful (http://about.com/webdesign/successfulsites). You can use those examples to improve your own site.

that to my site on About.com, which is primarily an information site with a narrower and deeper architecture. Both our sites have a slightly mixed focus, but we both understand the primary goals of our customers and base the site structure on that, rather than trying to mix it.

Wide and Shallow Sites

Wide and shallow sites have most of their links right on the home page. This site structure assumes that most people will start at the front page and move on to the topics or products of interest. It isn't as important in a wide-and-shallow site that the visitors move around through the site as it is that they find what they are looking for quickly and easily.

These sites have a structure that provides as much information as possible right at the first or second level of the site. Most sub-pages don't have a lot of pages underneath them because they provide all the information that your customers need right there. Wide and shallow sites have a structure that looks something like this:

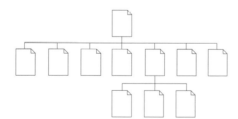

Figure 2-1: Wide and shallow site structure

You can use wide and shallow site structures whenever you have a goal of selling a few products or services. For example, sites that are focused on sales of a small set of products, sites that provide information on a limited number of topics (five to six), or

ASK YOUR GUIDE

Why do I need to worry about site structure right now?

▶ It's tempting to allow your Web site to grow organically, but that makes it harder for your customers. It also becomes more company focused, rather than customer focused. I worked on one site where all the site areas were named for code names that had no meaning to the customers. When we changed the site structure around and renamed site areas to match customer needs, more customers found the products they wanted, and we saw an upswing in sales. Site structure makes a difference.

sites with only ten to twenty pages work best with a wide and shallow site structure. If you don't have a lot of pages, there is no reason to divide them into categories and force your readers to click more.

Narrow and Deep Sites

Narrow and deep Web sites are larger and more categorized than wider sites. These are sites where it is important to show the depth of information available. This site structure assumes that customers will hit almost any page on the site, rather than just the home page. Navigation within the secondary pages becomes more important than the home page.

ELSEWHERE ON THE WEB

▶ There are many other types of site structure designs beyond the two I've mentioned in this book. The *Web Style Guide*, by Patrick Lynch and Sarah Horton (online at http://ftp. at.gnucash.org/languages/ html/webstyle), offers a nice description of several site structures. The most interesting one is the Web structure in which nearly all pages on the site link to each other.

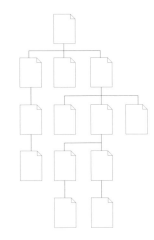

Figure 2-2: Narrow and deep site structure

Narrow and deep sites require more thought because they require more categorization. On my About.com site, I have been struggling with categorization almost as long as I've run the site. You would think that something like the category on learning HTML and Web design would have a standard title, but I've had to test several different categories before finding one that seems to work:

- Beginning HTML
- Learn HTML and Web Design
- HTML/**XHTML** Tutorials
- Web Design/HTML Tutorials
- Getting Started in Web Design/HTML

Narrow and deep sites have a structure that looks something like this:

Categorizing a narrow and deep site is crucial. If you don't have categories, then your customers won't find the content they need to find. There are several ways that you can determine the categories to use for your narrow and deep site:

- **Guess.** This is the least effective, but if you have no time or resources to spend on your categories, then it can work.
- **Guess and test.** Once you have some guesses as to the appropriate categories, test them with your customers. Provide users with a task and ask them what they would click on to do it. For example, on a dog toys site, you could ask them what they click on to find a toy for a poodle and see what they suggest.
- **Use your search logs.** Once your site has been up for a while, look at what search terms people use to find things on your site. Common terms should be categories.
- **Hire a librarian.** Library science is the study of organization systems, and hiring someone to help you determine a categorization scheme for your site is a great way to start. Chapter 15 can help you find outside help.

Narrow and deep site structures are used on sites with large amounts of information. They are best suited to sites with a broad topic with lots of subcategories, like the Web Design/HTML site at About.com or for product sites that have a large number of different types of products, such as a large online store like Amazon.com.

Narrow and deep sites can easily evolve out of a wide and shallow site. If you start out with only ten to twenty pages on your Web site, you should start with a wide and shallow structure. As you add more and more products, services, or information, you can add more categories and deepen your coverage.

Don't overcategorize. It's easy to fall into the trap of wanting to look bigger than you actually are, and many sites do this by overcategorizing their content. The more categories you have, the more your customers have to work to find what they're looking for. If you can get them to the information they want in one click, they will be happier and come back for more.

Standard Page Types

Most Web sites have five types of Web pages:

1. Content pages, which contain information
2. Product pages, which define the products that you sell
3. Information pages, which provide information about your Web site, your company, or yourself
4. Navigation pages, which get your customers from place to place
5. A home page, which has several uses, such as showcasing products and articles and providing links to press releases and PR materials

The following sections cover these different kinds of pages in more detail.

The goal of content pages is to provide your customers information about one topic. This could be anything from a fiction story to a nonfiction essay. If your site is focused on information delivery, then it will have content pages to provide that information. Content pages have the following characteristics:

- Information delivery is the goal of the page.
- There is a lot of text or descriptive imagery.
- Advertising is prominent.
- There will be a lot of links to related pages and other cat egories of interest.

Content pages are intended to provide information to your customers. The goal of the page is not to sell something, but to provide information to your customer so that he can do something. Content pages are most common on content-focused Web sites because they provide the information that these sites deliver. On my About.com site, every article that I write is a content page.

The content page delivers text or imagery. Some content pages will be shorter than others. For example, a glossary page might only have one or two sentences on it. The focus of the page is on the definition—the content of the page.

Advertising is prominent on a content page. Because the goal of the page is to provide information, advertising covers the costs of developing and delivering that information.

Related links and information will be found on nearly any page type, but on a content page they serve a second purpose of directing the readers to more information in the same category. The goal of a content site is to get people to read the content, so you want lots of links to content pages.

If your site is focused on selling products or services, then it will have product pages to provide information on what is for sale. Product pages have the following characteristics:

- Bulleted lists and short blocks of text provide information about the product.
- One large image of the product shows off what you are selling.
- Links on the page point to additional product information.
- The call to action promotes the sale in a prominent location on the page.

Unlike content pages, product pages are not very wordy. They have only enough information on the page to inform customers about the product and help them make the decision to purchase. Because the purpose of the page is to promote a sale, the text will be short and easy to read, usually in bulleted lists or very short paragraphs. A product page on my site looks like this: **http://about. com/webdesign/headrushajax**.

Images are important on product pages. They help customers recognize what they are buying. Even pages that are selling something that doesn't have a visual component will have an image to convey something about that product or service. The images serve the purpose of helping the customer decide to buy the item for sale.

Product pages have very few links on them. It's important to keep your customer on the page. In some cases, the product page will only have links to buy the product or get more information.

A product page must have a call to action. This is a link, form field, or phone number that prompts the customer to take action. After the product photo, this should be the most prominent element on the page. It entices customers to buy what you have for sale.

In Chapter 6 you will learn how to build a page to sell your products.

Information pages are similar to content pages because they have a lot of information. However, information pages are company-focused rather than customer-focused. Information pages have the following characteristics:

- The content is focused on the company rather than the customer.
- They include forms and contact information for the company.
- They are written in legalese.

The difference between an information page and a content page is the focus. They are built to promote the whole company, rather than a specific product or information.

"Contact Us" pages are information pages that allow your customers to interact directly with your company. The forms that you find on an information page are put there to request additional information rather than to promote a sale.

Many companies have legal documents that they are required to put online. Privacy policies, press releases, and user agreements all are found on the Web. They are required by government regulations or your legal department. They don't get a lot of page views but are important to your site. Chapter 7 explains how to create effective information pages.

Unless you can link all your pages from your home page, you'll need at least one or two navigation pages. The purpose of navigation pages is to direct customers to other locations on the site. Navigation pages have the following characteristics:

- Links are the content.
- Images are limited to icons and small photos.
- Text is limited to short paragraphs.
- Advertising and calls to action are less prominent.

Links are the purpose of navigation pages. Links get customers from one part of the site to another. Some navigation pages use long lists of links while others use shorter lists with descriptions.

Images are less important on navigation pages, unless they are used to help people find what they are looking for. The first page of most photo galleries is a navigation page that allows you to see all the photos at once and then go to the ones that look most interesting.

Text on navigation pages, outside of the links, is limited to describing the links and where they will go. The purpose of any additional text on the page is to encourage readers to click on the links.

Navigation pages don't have the goal of making money, so they don't need a lot of ads or buy links on them. It is common on sites that are funded by advertising to place ads on their navigation pages; the ads are secondary to the navigation links.

Chapter 8 explains how to create navigation pages including error message pages such as the "404: Page Not Found" page.

Home pages are special because they have to meet multiple goals. Content, product, and navigation pages have only one goal. Here are some goals of a home page:

- They showcase products and articles.
- They provide links to press releases and PR materials.
- They drive customers to promotions and specials.
- They include information about your company and your Web site.

In many cases, the goals for your home page can conflict with one another, which makes home-page design a challenge. If your company has more than one category or product line, the people responsible will want their categories on the home page, and as high up as possible. Because home pages are so important and so difficult to build, I have devoted all of Chapter 9 to helping you build a great home page for your site.

Decide on a Naming Convention Now

The final part of site structure is the naming convention used for files, folders, and **URLs**. Unfortunately, this is something that many companies never think about, or they think about it after the site has been built. If you wait to decide on a naming convention, you will have a lot of files, directories, and images that are incorrectly named.

When I was building my HTML Tags Library (**http://about.com/webdesign/htmltags**), I decided that I wanted to put the pages up with the word "tags" in the file name. I did this to make it easy to track the pages as a group. I named them all something like "bltags-a.htm." But with changes to the About.com systems, I had two problems:

- Hyphens were disallowed in file names.
- File names could only be 15 characters long.

I had to rename all the files to remove the hyphen and I had to shorten file names like "bltags-blockquote.htm" which were longer than the 15-character limit. This took me nearly three months to complete. If the naming conventions had been specified at the start, I wouldn't have had all that extra work.

As you read this book, you will be building a Web site along with me. I am building a Web site for my dogs. The goal of the site is to help provide more information about dogs and to sell the dog toys and equipment that my dogs prefer. The site will have content and product pages as well as information and category pages. It will be a small site so it will have a wide and shallow site structure. I've put a few mockups of how it will look on my About.com site: http://about.com/webdesign/mockups. I'll continue to reference this sample site throughout the rest of the book.

Start with directories. Directories are where your files are stored on the Web site. Refer to your plan from Chapter 1. What site elements do you want to have? The easiest way to name your directories is to use those planned site elements as your directory names. For example, in my sample site I will have the following directories:

```
Categories
  /breeds
  /health
  /photos

About This Site
  /about

Shared Content for the Entire Site
  /images
  /styles
  /scripts
```

In my sample site I'll sell dog toys. Since it's a smaller site than the information site there are fewer directories:

```
Products for sale
  /products

About this site
  /about

Shared content for the entire site
  /images
  /styles
  /scripts
```

Both sites have similar directory names for the shared content and information pages. The difference is in the categories and products sections. There are more categories in the information site because it is going to have extensive information about dogs. The products site is shallower because there are fewer pages and the goal is to sell dog toys rather than provide content.

Name your files sensibly. The problem I had with the naming convention on About.com was that we moved from a freeform system to a database-driven system, where there wasn't as much room for expansive file names. There are some simple things you can do to prevent problems with your file names:

- File names should not have any special characters. Limit your file names to letters, numbers, and underscores (_).
- Always put an extension on your files. For your Web pages, it should be .htm or .html. For images, use .gif or .jpg. For scripts and styles, use .js and .css respectively.
- Keep file names short. Fifteen to twenty characters, including the extension, is a good rule of thumb.
- Use words that are meaningful. Maintaining a Web site where all the pages bear a computer-generated name is impossible.

Document your naming convention. Having a naming convention is important, but it only works if you write it down.

Your documentation should include the following:

The item
- Directories
- HTML files
- Images
- Multimedia files

The naming convention
- Acceptable characters
- Length
- Special coding, such as date stamps or initial or final characters

Locations
- On the Web site
- Backups

WHAT'S HOT

▶ There is a lot more to building Web sites than HTML. There is also Flash (http://about.com/webdesign/flash), PHP (http://about.com/webdesign/php), and Java (http://about.com/webdesign/java). ASP and PHP are gaining popularity in the Windows and Linux communities respectively. If you don't know what those are, I've explained some of the more common in my article "Other Web Files" (http://about.com/webdesign/otherfiles).

Who can make changes to the naming convention

I use several naming conventions on the files on my About .com Web Design/HTML site. For example:

File Type	Naming Convention	Example
Article	Starts with "aa" followed by the date it was first published (MMDDYY). No special characters allowed. All lowercase. Maximum 15 characters long.	`aa102797.htm`
Glossary entry	Starts with "bldef" followed by as much of the word as possible. No special characters allowed. All lowercase. Maximum 15 characters long.	`bldefagent.htm`
HTML Tag	Starts with "bltags_" followed by as much of the tag name as possible. Other than the underscore, no special characters allowed. All lowercase. Maximum 15 characters long.	`bltags_var.htm`

File Type	Naming Convention	Example
Product Review	Starts with "aapr" followed by as much of the product name as possible. No special characters allowed. All lowercase. Maximum 15 characters long.	`aaprfirefoxsecr.htm`
Images for a product review	Starts with "aafr" followed by as much of the product name as possible. No special characters allowed. All lowercase. Maximum 15 characters long.	`aafrhdrushajax.jpg`

With my naming conventions written down, I am less likely to forget them, name files differently, and then lose the ability to manage them.

I also use the file names as additional information about the file. For example, naming articles with the date lets me know when they were written.

Use your file and directory names. File and directory names provide additional information about Web pages. Many Web logs use directory paths to show the date of a file. For example, an article written on October 27, 1997, could be stored in a directory structure like this:

```
/1997/10/27/index.html
```

The file could also be named `aa102797.htm`. Both methods provide the same information for about the same amount of work.

Get Linked

Site structure is an important part of a Web site. These links to my About.com site will help you go further in building your site structure and planning your site architecture.

INFORMATION ARCHITECTURE LINKS

There are a lot of resources and help for learning more about information architecture, and I've collected a few of the better ones on my site.

http://about.com/webdesign/infoarchitecture

TEN TIPS TO DRIVE AWAY YOUR READERS

When thinking about the site structure, keep these tips in mind. If you know what you shouldn't be doing, you'll be able to focus on all the things you should be doing.

http://about.com/webdesign/whatnottodo

SITE STRUCTURE LINKS

Building a site structure is crucial to making Web pages that are useful and interesting to your customers.

http://about.com/webdesign/sitestructure

Chapter 3

Hosting Your Web Site

Why Hosting Is Important

The way to understand Web hosting is to think of a Web page as an actual place, like your house. It has an address, the URL; it is made of building blocks, the HTML; and it has a physical location, the **hosting service provider**.

The problem for most beginners is that Web pages are viewed on your computer and when you start building them, you're building them on that same computer. Many beginning Web designers think that the Web pages they view in their browser are on the computer. But they aren't. When you visit a Web page, you aren't copying the Web pages from that URL to your computer; instead you are visiting the house of that Web page—in a completely different location. Your computer is the vehicle that drives you from one address (URL) to another. When you build a Web page, you need to put it up where other browsers can get to it. That place is your Web host.

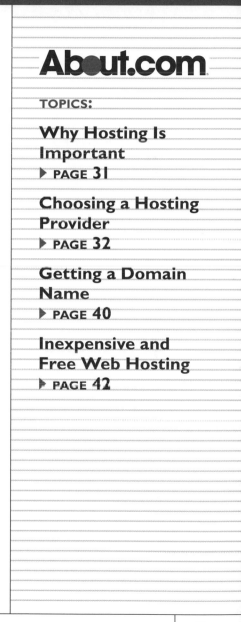

About.com

You need Web hosting to show your Web pages to other people. It is possible to create a Web page or even an entire site on your computer and never put it on a hosting provider. But then the only people who can see it are the people who can come and look at your computer. (Web sites called kiosks are built to be viewed in this way, but they are beyond the scope of this book.) A Web-hosting service provider gives your Web page an address or URL and a physical location.

Choosing the right Web host is important. It is possible to move a Web site from one hosting provider to another, but it can be very difficult. Unless you have a very small site with five or fewer pages and a few images, moving a Web site can be very onerous. It's much easier to find the right Web-hosting provider for your business and leave your site there.

I speak from experience. I moved a medium-sized small business site (around 500 pages) to three different hosting platforms before finding the one that worked best. Every move took the site down for at least a day, and content or programs (or both) were always missing on the new host and had to be rebuilt.

Choosing a Hosting Provider

As with Web-design software, price isn't the most important feature in your hosting service. You need to think of the bigger picture. You wouldn't buy a house based solely on price, and you shouldn't buy a house for your Web site on that basis either. If you're lucky, your Web site will live for many years at the hosting provider you choose now.

Ease of use is very important. The problem with this criterion is that it is difficult to know whether a hosting provider is difficult to use until you've used it.

In order to test a host, the best solution is to ask for a trial period. Then you can try building and maintaining one or two pages and find out how easy the providers you like are for you to use.

Before you decide, ask yourself these questions:

- How easy is it to get files up to the Web server?
- Will my Web-design software connect to their server?
- Is there a twenty-four-hour tech-support line available for me to call?
- Is that line toll-free or in a local calling zone?
- Does the provider offer extra services if I need them, such as **CGI** installation, server patches, or modules?
- Are those extra services within my budget?
- Are the online tools intuitive to me?
- Is there documentation for the tools and is it easy to understand?
- Are there user support groups or other interest groups who use the same hosting provider?
- Are there online forums I can access for help?

While not all of these options are required to make a hosting service provider easy to use, the more that are provided, the better. I have found that it's easier to get help from other people who use the same system than to try and go through the company's help pages. But this isn't a problem if the help is readily available.

Twenty-four-hour technical support is useful, especially at first. If you can't figure out how to get your Web site onto a host's servers, it's important to have someone to show you how. And the first time you have an access problem at 11 P.M. you'll appreciate an available tech-support person.

TOOLS YOU NEED

▶ If you're thinking of testing out a hosting provider and you can't decide if it's going to be easy to use, you can always ask people on the Web Design/HTML forums at http://about.com/web design/forums. It's easy to post your question there, and many people read the pages. Someone there may use the host you're considering. Plus, they may have suggestions for other hosts that meet your criteria.

Access to the site includes both virtual and physical access. Site access is how you post your pages and make changes. If you're using a colocation provider, you'll need physical access to your Web server. (The term "colocation" indicates a Web server that is owned by a company but hosted by a different company that provides the Internet access.)

In some corporations, for security reasons, the only place you can access the Web site is behind the corporate firewall. But other businesses need to have their site accessible wherever the Web developer is. This is especially true in a small business, where the Web developer might also be the lead sales person or even the CEO.

Security is important, and you should assess the needs of your company before you decide that you want to be able to access your Web site from anywhere. If you can access it, then hackers can, too. Don't assume that because a site is small it is safe. Most small companies don't do enough to protect their Web sites from hackers.

Most of the time, security for your Web site only requires creating strong passwords and changing them regularly (every one to three months). A strong password consists of at least eight characters and is not a word that would be included in a dictionary—it includes a combination of letters, numbers, and symbols. It is not based on your personal information.

If you create strong passwords for the accounts that access your Web site, you can have greater access to your Web site outside a firewall or other security devices. This makes access easier when you are the sole proprietor or need to be able to edit your Web site even from outside your offices.

I like to set up my Web sites so that I have access to them from nearly everywhere. If I find a problem with my Web site while I'm on vacation, I won't wait until I'm back to fix it. I deal with the secu-

ELSEWHERE ON THE WEB

▶ Staying secure can be a challenge for a small business, and keeping your Web site secure but manageable can be even harder. This article from Symantec on cybercrime prevention tips (www.symantec.com/avcenter/cybercrime/prevention.html) should help. It explains how to create strong passwords, stay current on patches, and configure your systems for security.

rity issues by using SSH and secureFTP to connect to my servers and I change my passwords regularly.

You need space for your Web pages. Space on a Web hosting computer is different from space on your personal hard drive. I had many Web developers offer to go out and buy another hard drive for the server, but it doesn't work that way. Web-server hard drives need to be more robust than your personal computer hard drives. If you think about it, it makes sense. A Web server is running twenty-four hours a day, seven days a week, and most of that time someone is accessing the Web-server hard drive. Your personal or work computer may be on all the time, but you're not working on the hard drive constantly, even if you are a workaholic. (Everyone sleeps sometime.) Even if your Web site doesn't get that much traffic, if you're on a shared hosting system, the rest of the system does—so you need a hard drive that can handle the load.

Secondly, a Web-server hard drive is usually not one hard drive. Most hosting providers use what is called a drive array, multiple disks that ensure data security and redundancy. If there's a problem with the data in part of the array, the Web server won't go down for more than a few seconds until the array can get the data back online. Some hosting services offer multiple disk arrays as a way to balance the load on the Web server as well. If there are a lot of people hitting the first disk, the second disk is brought online so that the Web site stays fast for everyone.

Be aware of how much space you need for your Web site. Keep in mind that if you're using 10GB today, you might need 100GB next year, or only 15GB. Take a look at your plan for your Web site and make an estimate about how much space you think you'll need in a year or two. Here are some good measures:

Site Element	Space Required	Typical Amount*	Growth Per Year
HTML	20–30KB per page	20–30 pages	24 pages (2 per month)
CSS	20–50KB per document	2–5 documents	
Images	30–50KB per image	2–5 images per Web page	48–60 new images
Multimedia	40–50KB per document	Depends upon the site**	Depends upon the site**
Scripts	10–20KB per script	5–10 scripts	6–12 new scripts

*Most small businesses start out in this range for Web pages, CSS, images, and scripts.

**Multimedia uses a lot of space, but not all sites require it. If your site needs a PDF for every product, you will need more space than a site that only has one Flash demonstration.

WHAT'S HOT

▶ Some providers charge based on your average use. If your site suddenly sees a spike in page views, that can cause a lot of problems for the hosting provider. So, rather than charge you for the month's bandwidth, you may be charged for spikes in your traffic, even if your entire month's traffic is lower than your limit. This is explained in my article "Colocation Bandwidth Billing" (http://about.com/web design/bandwidthbilling).

Plan your space needs wisely. It is harder to start out with a large amount of space. I have found that many Web developers, when presented with a large amount of space, take it as a challenge to see how fast they can fill it. Just because you have 10 or 100GB of space right now doesn't mean that you should create images that are 10 or 100MB to fill it. If you're miserly with your space, your customers will thank you because your Web pages will download quickly. And your bottom line will thank you, as you won't be spending more and more money on space and **bandwidth** charges for your Web site.

Keep aware of bandwidth limits. These can be a huge source of income for your hosting provider and a large cash outflow for you. It's very important that you know if your hosting provider charges for bandwidth overages or has bandwidth limits.

Bandwidth is the measure of how much traffic your Web site is getting, multiplied by the amount of data that is being sent out. For example, if you have one Web page that is 1KB in size and it has no images, scripts, or external CSS files associated with it, then every time someone hits that page, you'll see a bandwidth transfer of 1KB. Most hosting providers have bandwidth limits and will charge more once you've reached your maximum bandwidth.

Remember that bandwidth is not just the size of your Web pages and images. It is also the number of hits to your site. The example site above might have a bandwidth usage of 1GB per month if enough people hit that one Web page. So even if your Web site is small, it might need a lot of bandwidth if it becomes popular. For a beginning site, bandwidth limits won't matter too much, but be aware of your provider's policy so that you're not stuck with a huge bill when your site hits the big time.

Don't overlook the hosting tools. It's good to know what tools you'll have available for your Web site if you ever need them. Some of the most common tools you'll find are these:

- FTP and file management software to transfer files to your site
- CGI access to write programs on the Web server
- Pre-built Web programs like **blogs**, calendars, forums, and chat rooms
- Log analysis tools to help you trace your page views

It can be easy to get swept up in the hype of a hosting provider's file management system that will do it all for you, but if you have FTP software, you may not need that tool, and it may even get in the way of maintaining your Web site. The same is true for items like CGI or prebuilt programs. If you don't think you'll be using them on your Web site, then why pay extra for the features?

When I'm looking at a hosting provider, I want a few specific tools:

- Shell access to my Web site is the most important thing. Then I can test programs and make changes directly on the server if I have to.
- FTP access to my Web site is also very important. I don't want to be forced to use a Web-based file transfer utility, as that can slow things down.
- CGI support for my site lets me use programs. I write my own programs or get prebuilt programs from other sites on the Web.

The server operating system matters when choosing a hosting provider. It doesn't have to match the operating system of your machine, but it should be an OS that offers what you need for your Web site.

ELSEWHERE ON THE WEB

▶ If you're interested in CGI scripts for your Web server, one of my favorite places to get them is the CGI Resource Index (http://cgi. resourceindex.com). This site offers many programs in different categories. It even has listings of developers who can build your CGI scripts for you.

OS	Benefits	Drawbacks
Linux	The most common server OS. Offers CGI scripts. There is a lot of help for maintaining sites on Linux servers.	If you're not familiar with Unix file systems, it can be hard to learn. For example, Linux file names are case sensitive while in Windows they are not.
Macintosh	Good Java support. The Macintosh OS is Unix and has all the same features as *nix systems.	Very hard to find.

OS	Benefits	Drawbacks
Unix	Very secure.	Difficult to use, similar to Linux systems. Can be expensive and hard to find.
Windows	ASP support. Familiar interface.	Not as common as Linux. Many security issues.

The type of hosting provider can make a difference too. The most common type of hosting provider is a basic Web hosting provider. They give you the following:

- Space on a server
- A specific URL that points to your Web site
- Access to the Web server, usually by FTP or shell

To build a Web site, all you need is a basic Web-hosting provider. You may find that your Internet service provider (ISP) can provide you with hosting that meets your business needs. The biggest benefit to an ISP hosting plan is that they are usually free with your Internet service. The drawbacks are that they have very small space and bandwidth limits and your URL will be something long and hard to remember.

If you're going to use your ISP as a hosting provider, then consider a domain host as well. Domain hosts point a domain name that you have purchased to your ISP URL.

Colocation is another choice in Web hosting. Instead of relying on your hosting provider to give you space on a server, you provide the server (and the space) yourself. What you pay for is to connect your hardware into their Internet access. Colocation is a great choice for a company that wants to have complete control over its Web site. With colocation, you control the server hardware, the operating system, the Web server software, and any other

TOOLS YOU NEED

▶ Deciding what operating system to use for your Web server can be hard. Linux is the most common Web hosting server OS out there, but that doesn't mean that it's the best one for your needs. My article "Windows versus Linux for Web Page Hosting" (http://about.com/webdesign/windowsvslinux) explains the differences between the various OSs and how to choose the right one for you.

applications you may want to run on your Web site. Your hosting provider gives you rack space to place your server on the network and a connection to the Internet. Some colocation providers also offer rentals of servers and the rack. This is called managed hosting. They maintain the hardware and software and you put your site on it. This is a good option if you don't want to maintain the server but you don't want your site hosted on a shared hosting provider.

It is hard to decide on a hosting solution. But it all comes back to your original plan for your Web site. Answer the following questions based on your plan for your Web site, and then you can compare the different hosting solutions:

- How big (in space usage) do I expect my site to be now? In one year? In five years?
- Do I need special programs to run on my site, such as PHP, CGI, ASP, JSP, or ColdFusion?
- Do I anticipate that my site will have large spikes of traffic, or will the page views be steady from week to week?
- How much control do I need over my Web-site hardware and software?
- How much am I willing to pay for my Web-site hosting?

Once you know the answers to those questions, check out Web hosting companies. A great place to start is my Web hosting list on my About.com site, at http://about.com/webdesign/webhosting.

Getting a Domain Name

Domain names are critical for Web businesses. While it is possible to run a Web business from a free Web site with an ugly URL, the most successful businesses have a domain name that relates to their business or their brand.

WHAT'S HOT

▶ If you're considering using your ISP for a hosting pro-vider and you're not sure what your URL is going to be, take a look at other Web pages that your ISP hosts. Typically, they have the ISP name at the beginning, and then a tilde, and then the login name. For example, my personal site on Netcom had the URL www.netcom.com/ ~jkyrnin (it doesn't exist any longer). My article "What's My URL?" (http://about.com/ webdesign/myurl) describes how to figure out what your URL is or will be.

Step 1: Choose your domain name provider. There are a lot of domain name providers to choose from, and you can choose based on price or availability. Some of the more popular domain name providers are the following:

- GoDaddy: www.godaddy.com
- Network Solutions: www.networksolutions.com
- Register.com: www.register.com
- Whois.com: www.whois.com
- directNIC: www.directnic.com

I use Network Solutions, the oldest and best-known domain provider. One-year registrations are more expensive than other services, but for longer terms they are competitive. I like their services and they make it easy to find available domain names.

Step 2: Choose your domain name. Chances are good that someone else has taken your first choice of domain name. The domain provider will help you choose another name, either with similar wording or a different extension (instead of .com you could have .net or .org, for example). You want a domain name that represents your company, is easy to remember and type, and won't be confused with something else.

Purchase your domain. I buy domains for ten years so that I don't have to worry about them for a long time. The cost is around $10 to $25 a year for ten years and is a minimal expense for most businesses. Purchasing your domain from a low-cost domain host may seem like a good way to save money, but it can cost you in the long run. Domain registrars have gone out of business, leaving the domains they registered in limbo. Make sure, if you go with a low-cost registrar, that you are purchasing full rights to your domain, not just

ASK YOUR GUIDE

Colocation sounds expensive. Why would I choose it?

▶ I have been using colocation services for nearly three years, and I love it. Colocation gives you much more control over your Web server and what's on it than any other hosting type. I like that I can control who sees my site, what they see, and what is hosted there without having to work with any support people. And my Web servers are served on T3 connections, which make them very fast.

the billing information. This includes technical and administrative contacts on the domain. Make sure you can change registrars if you decide to later.

I never purchase the "unlimited" or 100-year domain registrations. While the cost per year may be a lot lower, not a lot of businesses have been around for more than 100 years.

Inexpensive and Free Web Hosting

Unlike your Web-design software, it is possible to be more frugal with your hosting options and still maintain a great Web site for your business. The key is to know what to keep.

Use your ISP. Especially when you first start out, you don't need much space for your Web site, so using your ISP is a great way to get your business on the Web without spending a lot of money on hosting. Check with your Internet service provider; many plans include space on their servers for you to put up a Web site.

If your ISP doesn't offer free Web hosting, then go to a free Web-hosting site like GeoCities or Tripod. I list a few of the better ones on my site (**http://about.com/webdesign/freewebhosting**). The problem with these free sites is that you pay for them through advertising that is placed on your Web sites. This can affect the layout and design of your site as well as distract your customers.

Purchase a domain name for ten years or more. In the long run, $150 to $250 is not a lot of money to a business, large or small. And if you purchase your domain over longer periods of time, most domain registrars will give you a discount on the annual cost. You gain several benefits from doing this.

- You get a discount on the annual fee.
- No one can use that domain for as long as you own it.

- You can sell it to someone else during that time frame.
- You don't have to renew the domain every year.

Forward your domain. Once you have your Web site up on your ISP, then buy a domain name. But instead of using the hosting options that they offer, forward the domain to your free Web site (such as the one on your ISP). Domain forwarding tells the Internet that when a request comes in for your purchased domain, the pages hosted on your free URL should be displayed.

Research and plan for the future. Chances are, you'll eventually need to move your Web site away from your ISP to a more conventional hosting alternative. Ideally, moving your site means zipping the site on your old server and then unzipping it on the new one. But it is almost never that easy. Some hosting services don't provide access to zip your files (or unzip them). And if you're moving from one operating system to another, the transfer may have additional problems. Plan ahead by taking the following steps:

- Keep your site up to date. If you have to move, you won't be able to maintain your site during the move. If it's up to date, the disruption won't be as noticeable.
- Delete files you are no longer linking to or using.
- Keep a backup of your Web site on your local hard drive.
- Keep track of the files that are server dependent, like CGI and PHP scripts.
- Document your file system (naming conventions, file folder names and locations, and any special features of your site).

Finding the right hosting solution for your Web site can save you headaches in the future.

ELSEWHERE ON THE WEB

▸ Be sure to test your idea for a domain name with other people before you buy it. While it may make perfect sense to you, the way domain names are written can result in some unintentionally funny misunderstandings. The article "The Top Ten Unintentionally Worst Company URLs" (http://independent sources.com/2006/07/12/worst-company-urls) lists some bad domain names.

Get Linked

Hosting can be a very complex topic, and there are a lot of resources out there to help you find the perfect hosting provider.

WHAT IS COLOCATION AND WHY WOULD YOU CHOOSE IT FOR WEB HOSTING?

Many small businesses don't realize that they can have the same options for their Web servers as larger businesses if they choose to use colocation rather than an externally hosted solution. This article series on colocation covers all you need to know to make that decision.

http://about.com/webdesign/colocation

BEFORE YOU BUY WEB HOSTING

If you're looking for a quick overview of Web hosting and your options, this article should help. It covers the basics of Web hosting and provides some suggestions for how to get the right hosting for you.

http://about.com/webdesign/bybwebhosting

Chapter 4

All about Code

Deciding What Code You Need

It's important that Web designers have at least a minimal under-standing of the HTML code that is needed for the building of a Web page. While there are Web-page editors out there that don't allow you to look at the code, let alone edit it, most professional Web sites are not built with them. Until the tools and standards are more in sync, it's important that you know a little HTML.

Luckily, HTML isn't hard. Unluckily, there are many other lan-guages you can learn to build a top-quality Web site. And some of them are quite hard.

HTML is just one type of Web code. While the basis of a Web page is HTML, several other languages are also used to build Web pages, including these:

- (X)HTML
- ASP

About.com

- ColdFusion
- JSP
- PHP

HTML (also called XHTML) stands for HyperText Markup Language (the X in XHTML stands for eXtensible). It is the basic building block of a Web page.

Plain HTML is all you need. All those other languages are useful and serve a purpose, but they can be very advanced and difficult to learn. It's easy to get excited at the idea of a database-driven Web site with lots of programming and dynamic action, but all you need is HTML (and some CSS). After reading this book, you will have learned enough HTML and CSS to build a Web site without using any other advanced languages.

What about JavaScript? JavaScript is a special case. It is a client-side programming language that allows you to do exciting things on your Web pages. This language is so robust that there are many books available on writing great JavaScript. The About.com JavaScript Guide has a lot of information on the topic on his site (http://javascript.about.com). In this book, I'll give you some simple scripts for your Web site, but for more advanced training, see the About.com JavaScript Web site.

Use other languages when it makes sense. Beginning Web designers can get so carried away with technology that their Web pages become a hodge-podge of styles, designs, scripts, animations, and insanity. Web technology follows a hierarchy. Don't move up the ladder if you can solve your problem using the lowest rung of the hierarchy:

ELSEWHERE ON THE WEB

▶ If you want to add some PHP, JSP, or ASP to your Web sites, there are sites on About.com that cover these topics in more detail. There is an entire Guide site on PHP and mySQL (http://php .about.com). The About.com Java Guide has a section devoted to JSP and Java Web programming (http://about .com/java/javawebprogram).

- **Level 1: HTML**—HTML is the basis of all Web pages. You might be surprised at what you can do with just a few HTML tags. This is where to start when solving a problem for the Web.
- **Level 2: CSS**—CSS or **cascading style sheets** create the look and feel of your Web pages. If HTML is the structure of your pages, then CSS is the floor plan and the color scheme. Look to CSS second for solving Web problems.
- **Level 3: Client-side scripts**—JavaScript, ActiveX, and other client-side scripts provide you with a lot of flexibility on Web pages. These don't interact with the Web server directly and are less intrusive. JavaScript is the third step in solving Web problems.
- **Level 4: Web applications**—Flash, **applets**, and objects all add more functionality to your Web pages, but at the expense of usability and **accessibility**. They are harder on the server and systems and should be looked at fourth when solving Web problems.
- **Level 5: Server-side scripts**—These are programming languages like JSP, ASP, Perl, and PHP. They run on the Web server. They require more knowledge to develop and should be looked at last when solving Web problems.

I'll go into more detail about advanced technology in Chapter 14.

HTML to Start With

There are hundreds of HTML tags that you can use to build a Web page, but you may be surprised to learn that most Web sites only use a small fraction of the available tags. You can build a Web site with only six types of tags:

TOOLS YOU NEED

▶ If you're still determined to use the latest and greatest Web technology, then read my article "Designing Cutting Edge Web Sites" (http://about.com/webdesign/cutingedge). It poses four questions to ask yourself about the technology to determine if it is best for your customers or just for your ego.

I'm using a WYSIWYG editor. Why do I need to know HTML?

▶ You may be surprised at how easy it is to learn HTML. You can build a high-quality Web site using only about twenty tags. If you can learn those tags, you can then use your WYSIWYG editor for what it's good at: helping you to visualize the styles that you apply to your HTML.

- Structural tags
- Text tags
- List tags
- Image tags
- Link tags
- Layout tags

Many of those tag categories have only one HTML **element** that you should learn to use.

But before we learn about the specific tags, let's talk about HTML. In this book, I will be teaching you valid XHTML, an advanced version of HTML. I will use the terms XHTML and HTML interchangeably throughout the rest of the text. Make sure you obey the following rules when writing your HTML:

- HTML is a text language. You can't use programs like Microsoft Word to write HTML. Use an HTML editor or text editor only.
- Valid XHTML is all lower case.
- HTML is made up of elements (also called tags) and **attributes** of those elements.
- Elements are surrounded by angle brackets < and >.
- The first word after the initial angle bracket is the tag. For example, `<strong>`—strong is the element name.
- Attributes are included after a space following the tag. The name of the attribute is given first, then an equal sign, then the value of the attribute in quotation marks. For example, the attribute href would be coded like so: `<a href="http://webdesign.about.com/">`—href="http://webdesign.about.com/" is the attribute.

Elements always have a start tag and an end tag.

- The end tag will match the start tag but with a slash after the first angle bracket, like so: `</strong>`.
- Text enclosed between the two tags is affected by that element. For example, text surrounded by an `<a>` tag will be linked. In `<a href="http://webdesign.about.com/">About.com Web Design/HTML</a>`—"About.com Web Design/HTML" is the linked text.
- Some tags don't enclose any text, and so the end tag can be collapsed into the start tag. For example, a line break is written: `<br/>`.

Structural tags are the backbone of your HTML document. These are the tags that tell the Web browser that it's displaying a Web page and not a PDF or other document. Every Web page should have structural elements in the document.

`<html> . . . </html>`
This is the outermost element in an HTML document. The `<html>` tag should be the first tag on your Web page, and the `</html>` tag should be the last.

`<head> . . . </head>`
The head of an HTML document contains information about the Web page that won't be shown on the page. This includes things like the title, links to CSS and scripts, and meta data.

`<title> . . . </title>`
This tag identifies the title of the Web page. This is what is displayed in search engine results, bookmarks, and in the Web-browser title bar.

WHAT'S HOT

▶ You may think you know what text is, but if you're only familiar with Word documents you don't. Text to a computer is different than letters on the screen, and most programs (not Web editors) that allow you to write text on a computer are writing rich text. Rich text is text with formatting built in. Web pages are text without formatting. My article "What Is Text and What Is a Text Editor?" (http://about.com /webdesign/whatistext) explains the difference.

Figure 4-1: The Web browser title bar in Firefox

WHAT'S HOT

▶ The DOCTYPE tag is more important than you may realize, as Web browsers behave differently depending upon which you use. If you're designing a page to look the same in multiple browsers, you must use a doctype. If you don't, browsers display the page in what is called quirks mode. Learn more about quirks mode on my site (http://about. com/webdesign/quirksmode) or about the DOCTYPE tag in general (http://about.com/ webdesign/doctype).

`<meta />`
Meta tags are used to define information about the page. The two types of meta tags we'll use on our Web site are for search engine optimization: keywords and description.

`<link />`
The link tag allows you to connect CSS style sheets to your HTML.

`<body> . . . </body>`
The body element contains everything that shows up on your Web page.

Web pages should also have the **DOCTYPE** element. Technically, DOCTYPE is not an HTML element, but rather a declaration that tells the browser what version of XHTML or HTML the page is written in. For our Web sites, we'll be using the XHTML 1.0 Transitional DOCTYPE, coded like so:

```
<!DOCTYPE html PUBLIC "-//W3C//DTD XHTML 1.0
Transitional//EN"
"http://www.w3.org/TR/xhtml1/DTD/xhtml1-transi-
tional.dtd">
```

Putting these tags together, you would have a functional (but completely blank) Web page. For my sample site, I would put them together like this:

```
<!DOCTYPE html PUBLIC "-//W3C//DTD XHTML 1.0
Transitional//EN"
"http://www.w3.org/TR/xhtml1/DTD/xhtml1-transi-
tional.dtd">
<html>
<head>
<title>Dogs and Their Toys</title>
<meta name="description" content="Great dog toys
that your dogs will love and information about
dogs." />
<meta name="keywords" content="dogs, dog toys,
canines, information about dogs, dog help" />
</head>
<body>
</body>
</html>
```

To create your Web page, copy the code above exactly as it is written. Then you can change the text inside the title, meta description, and meta keywords to reflect the content of your site. Save your Web page to a new folder on your hard drive called MyWebSite and name the page page1.html. Once you've saved the file to your hard drive, you can view it with your Web browser. Open your Web browser and click on "File" and then "Open" or "Open File . . ." and browse to the page you just saved. Remember that because there is nothing inside the body element, the page will be blank in your browser. All that should display is the title in the title bar.

If you don't want to type the HTML into your editor, you can find the code online at **http://about.com/webdesign/example 4-1code**. The page itself is online at **http://about.com/webdesign/ example4-1page** (blank, just like yours will be).

Text tags are the tags that define your content. These are tags for paragraphs, line breaks, and tags for headings, strong, and emphasis. They provide some definition to your text.

In valid XHTML, HTML tags are not used to describe what your page will look like. Instead, the appearance of text is defined semantically. For example, the text you're reading here is in a paragraph, so it would be enclosed in a paragraph element. I would use the CSS, rather than HTML, to make the paragraph large, red, and bold.

We'll use the following HTML text tags:

```
<p> . . . </p>
```
The paragraph tag: All text that is in a paragraph should be enclosed in this element, one paragraph per element.

```
<br />
```
The line break tag: This element separates the text into two lines on the Web page, one before and one after the element.

```
<h1> . . . </h1> <h2> . . . </h2> <h3> . . . </h3>
```
Heading tags: The h1 tag is the most important heading on the page, h2 is the second most important, and h3 is the third most important. HTML allows up to six levels of headings.

```
<strong> . . . </strong> <em> . . . </em>
```
Strong and emphasis tags: These tags tell the browser that the enclosed text has a stronger or more emphasized tone to it. While browsers have standard ways of displaying strong and emphasized text (usually bold and italicized, respectively), we will be using CSS to define exactly how we want these tags to look.

```
<blockquote> . . . </blockquote>
```
Tag used to define quotation: The blockquote tag is used to call out text that is quoted.

We can add these tags to our Web site—and this is where we add content to the Web page. All text elements are enclosed in the <body> element, as you can see below.

```
<!DOCTYPE html PUBLIC "-//W3C//DTD XHTML 1.0
Transitional//EN"
"http://www.w3.org/TR/xhtml1/DTD/xhtml1-
transitional.dtd">
<html>
<head>
<title>Dogs and Their Toys</title>
<meta name="description" content="Great dog toys
that your dogs will love and information about
dogs." />
<meta name="keywords" content-"dogs, dog toys,
canines, information about dogs, dog help" />
</head>
<body>
<h1>Dogs and Their Toys</h1>
<p>
My two dogs would like to share their special
knowledge of dog toys. In the course of their
life they have tried out numerous dog toys and
found that some work better than others.
</p>
<h2>Who Are the Dogs?</h2>
<p>
<strong>Shasta</strong> - a 6-year-old
<em>mutt</em><br />
<strong>McKinley</strong> - a 1-year-old
<em>Border collie</em>
</p>
<p>McKinley says:</p>
<blockquote>I like dog toys that are soft and
easy to rip up. They call me the Doctor, because
I like to surgically remove the squeakers.</
blockquote>
```

```
<p>Shasta says:</p>
<blockquote>My favorite dog toy is McKinley,
because any toy I play with he steals from me.
But if I had to choose, I'd pick the big fluffy
balls.</blockquote>
</body>
</html>
```

As you can see, I've added all of these new tags (and their corresponding text) in between the `<body>` and `</body>` tags. When you look at the page in a Web browser you can see that it isn't very pretty, but the content all shows up.

Try adding your own paragraphs, headings, and quotations to your Web page. The HTML is available online (**http://about.com/ webdesign/example4-2code**).

List tags are for lists of items. Lists are important because even though they aren't always formatted (using CSS) with bullets, most of the things we deal with on Web pages are lists. A Web site might feature the following lists:

- Site navigation
- Products available for sale
- Contact and mailing addresses
- Articles on the site
- Links to related Web sites

On many Web sites, you'll see designers write lists as paragraphs, tables, divisions, or lines of text separated by a <br />. This is incorrect. Instead use a list element:

```
<li> . . . </li>
```

This tag is for the list item itself. Every item in a list should be enclosed in this element.

```
<ul> . . . </ul>
```

This tag is used for an unordered list, where elements have no intrinsic order. This is the standard bulleted list. The only elements inside a <ul> element are the <li> list elements themselves.

```
<ol> . . . </ol>
```

This tag is used for an ordered (or numbered) list, where elements go in a specific order. Just like the <ul> element, only <li> elements are allowed inside of it.

My example page does include a list: my dogs' names. In the first version of the page, I used <p> and <br /> tags to display the list, but to be more correct, I should convert them to a list:

```
<ul>
<li><strong>Shasta</strong> - a 6-year-old
<em>mutt</em></li>
<li><strong>McKinley</strong> - a 1-year-old
<em>Border collie</em></li>
</ul>
```

I can use an ordered list for the dog's favorite toys (**http://about .com/webdesign/example4-3**):

```
<ol>
<li>Soft squeak toys</li>
<li>Any toy Shasta has</li>
<li>Squeaky tennis balls</li>
</ol>
```

Another form of list is the definition list. Definition lists have three elements <dl>, <dt>, and <dd>. Use a definition list when you have items that consist of a word or phrase and then a definition. Instead of an ordered list for the dogs, I can use a definition list:

```
<dl>
<dt><strong>Shasta</strong></dt>
<dd>a 6-year-old <em>mutt</em></dd >
<dt><strong>McKinley</strong></dt>
<dd>a 1-year-old <em>Border collie
</em></dd>
</dl>
```

WHAT'S HOT

▶ My short article "Web Images Should Be Small" (http://about.com/webdesign/smallimages) can get you started creating images that are small and download quickly. I also go over this in more detail in Chapter 12.

Add graphics to your page with image tags. Images are very popular on Web pages. Here are some things to keep in mind when you're planning on using a graphic on a Web page:

- **Keep your graphics small.** Large images can make a page take forever to download.
- **Don't use graphics where you could use text or CSS.** Graphics should be considered one tool in your Web toolkit, not the only tool you have. This is especially true for text. If you have to type something into your image, consider making it HTML and styling it with CSS. Not only will your page load faster, text can be read by search engines while images can't.
- **Don't use graphics for layout.** A spacer **GIF** used to be the popular way to position other elements exactly where you wanted them on the page. But CSS allows you more precise control over your layout.

On the sample Web site, I'll add two photos (saved in JPG format) of the two dogs. The HTML I've added looks like this:

```
<p>
<img src="mckinley.jpg" alt="McKinley"
width="200" height="150" />
McKinley says:</p>
<blockquote>I like dog toys that are soft and
easy to rip up. They call me the Doctor, because
```

```
I like to surgically remove the squeakers.</
blockquote>
<p>
<img src="shasta.jpg" alt="Shasta" width="200"
height="150" />
Shasta says:</p>
```

As you can see from the HTML, the image tag is both a single-ton tag and has several attributes.

```
<img src="shasta.jpgv alt="Shasta" width="200"
height-"150" />
```

There are four attributes on my image elements, two required and two recommended:

src

The src attribute defines the source location of the image. This is the URL where the image is located on the Web server. This attribute is required.

alt

The alt attribute defines alternate text that should be displayed if the image does not appear. This is also required for valid XHTML and is a good idea to make your site accessible and search-engine friendly.

width

The width attribute defines the width of your images so that the browser can render the page more quickly. You can use this to resize the image, but that isn't recommended, as it will slow down the page load times and browsers don't do a good job at resizing images.

`height`

The height attribute defines the height of your images so that the browser can render the page more quickly. As with the width, you can use it to resize your images, but it's not a good idea.

My original images were both over 1000 pixels wide when I opened them in my graphics editor. So I cropped them to get just the dogs' faces and then I resized them so that they would fit better on the Web page. At 2.7 and 3.3 KB apiece, they won't impact the download of the page significantly.

ELSEWHERE ON THE WEB

▶ But what if you don't have an image-editing software tool to resize your images? After all, I did say that it wasn't absolutely required to put up a Web page. Well, it's a good idea to have your own image-editing tool, but if you don't have one, you can still resize and crop your images online, using the Online Image Resizer (www .resize2mail.com).

Figure 4-2: A very basic page with images

Link tags move your readers from place to place. Links or anchor tags point your readers to other places.

It's a good idea to have a linking strategy. Your linking strategy determines what types of sites you will link to, from what pages on your site, and if you have any special indications when you link to external sites or types of documents (such as PDF files or e-mail links). For example, the linking strategy I use on my About.com site looks something like this:

- I link to pages that are directly related to Web design, HTML, or XML concepts.
- I link deeply. Instead of pointing to the home page of a site, I link directly to the item of interest to my readers.
- I link to external pages only from my home-page blog or from category pages.
- External links are displayed differently from internal links on category pages.
- I prefer to link to HTML documents than to PDF or text.

Go and write your link strategy for your Web site right now. Since we're building a small business site, it's a good idea to limit your external links to one or two pages on your Web site, or even disallow them completely. For now, you don't need to differentiate between types of links or whether they are internal or external. Once you have your linking strategy, you'll be ready to learn how to add a link to your Web page.

You need to learn only one tag, with one attribute, to add links to your HTML:

```
<a href="http://webdesign.about.com/"> . . . </a>
```

Everything within the <a> tag will be part of the link, and you can link images or text in HTML documents.

For my Web page, I added some navigation. Since the other parts of the site don't exist yet, I left the href attribute blank, but the links will still show up on the Web page. Here's the HTML I added:

```
<ul>
<li><a href="">Home</a></li>
<li><a href="">Dog Toys for Sale</a></li>
<li><a href="">Dog Information</a></li>
<li><a href="">About This Site</a></li>
</ul>
```

Once I know what the URLs will be for my home page, dog toys category page, dog articles category page, and my information page, I can add them into the Web site.

The last type of tag you'll need for your site is a division tag. The division tag is used to divide up a page into segments so that they can be styled more easily. Be careful with your divisions. Only put them in your document where it makes sense to have them. Extra divisions make your pages longer to download. The tag for divisions is as follows:

```
<div> . . . </div>
```

When you add a division to a Web page without any styles, it won't appear to do much. An extra space may appear on the page (or it may not), but otherwise, your Web browser may ignore the <div> tags. This is okay. We are putting them into the document so that the style sheet has something to style when we start building the page.

Pages on my dog toys Web site will have three sections:

- The branding section at the top, which includes the headline, but doesn't include the navigation
- The body section currently in the middle of the page, which includes all of my text

- A new information section that will be at the bottom that includes things like my copyright

Because I want to style these sections, I will use an id attribute to name them in the HTML. You can only use an id once per page. If I have a "main" id, I can't use it a second time on another element. Since I'm giving my divisions ids, I will also identify my navigation list so that it is distinguishable (by the CSS) from any other lists on the page.

Here's the HTML for my branding division and my navigation list:

```
<div id="branding"><h1>Dogs and Their Toys</h1></div>
<ul id="navigation">
<li><a href="" >Home</a></li>
<li><a href="" >Dog Toys for Sale</a></li>
<li><a href="" >Dog Information</a></li>
<li><a href="" >About This Site</a></li>
</ul>
```

As you can see, all I did was surround my <h1> tag with a <div> tag and add the attribute id="navigation" to the <ul> tag.

You can see the additional div tags in the HTML on my Web site (http://about.com/webdesign/example4-6).

Adding Styles with CSS

Okay, I admit it: The page is ugly. So how can I be advocating a Web page that looks that ugly, plain, and boring in a Web design book?

Well, there are three parts to a Web page:

- The Web-page structure
- The Web-page look or style
- The Web-page behavior

The structure of the Web page is what we've built so far. It has content and HTML tags, but the styles are completely dependent upon the Web browser that is viewing the page.

CSS to the rescue. Cascading style sheets are what make our Web pages look nice. Many people think of them only as a way to change the **font**, but you can also use them to adjust the layout, modify how specific elements are displayed, and even hide elements if you don't want them visible.

The most efficient way to use style sheets is through an external style sheet. Then you can use the same styles on every Web page on your site if you want to. Here's how to link to your style sheet:

1. Open a new blank document in your HTML editor. If you have the option to open a new CSS file, do so.
2. Save the file in the same directory as your HTML file.
3. Name the file `styles.css`.
4. Open your HTML file in your editor.
5. Add the following line anywhere inside the `<head>` `</head>` element on your Web page:

```
<link type="text/css" href="styles.css"
rel="stylesheet" />
```

Some basic styles for your page. There are a lot of things we can do with style sheets, and we'll go into a lot more detail later on

▶ There are lots of other HTML elements that you can learn to enhance your Web site. This chapter only scratches the surface of available HTML tags. If you want to learn more HTML, the best way to do that is with my Free HTML class (http://about.com/webdesign/html course). In the class you will learn all the above HTML tags and many others, and you'll be able to apply them all even if you never touch a WYSIWYG editor.

in the book, but for now let's clean up some of the layout issues on the Web page and make the fonts and images look nicer.

The page is too wide.

Right now, the page doesn't have any page width set on it, so the text spans the entire width of the browser. That's fine if your browser is narrow, but on wider monitors and windows, the page will be hard to read. To fix that we need to set some margins on the page as a whole and set a width on the body tag. (Note that some browsers don't handle widths on the body tag well; we'll fix that in Chapter 5.)

In your styles.css document, type:

```
html, body { margin: 10px; }
body { width : 600px; }
```

The font for the entire page is ugly.

Now we're going to edit the body style to add some font information. (Don't worry if this is coming too quickly. We'll go over the specifics of CSS in later chapters.)

Change the body line to read:

```
body { width : 600px; font: normal 1em Geneva,
Arial, Helvetica; }
```

The images don't nest well in the document.

Float them to the left so that the text flows around them.

Add this line to your style sheet:

```
img { float : left; clear: both; margin: 0 10px
10px 0; }
```

Now even more of the text is to the right of the images than I wanted.

Figure 4-3: The <h3> headline is to the right of the image

To fix this, I added the following line:

```
h1,h2,h3 { clear : both; }
```

There's no color on the page.

I created a colored background to highlight the 700-pixel-wide column of text we created with our first styles.

```
html { background-color : #3c6; }
```

I want the information section to be less important.

I made the font a little smaller.

```
#information { font-size: .8em; }
```

You can see the finished page on the About.com Web Design site (http://about.com/webdesign/example4-8page). There is still a lot we can do to it, but it looks a lot more appealing now than it did when we first started. The final HTML and CSS are listed online as well (http://about.com/webdesign/example4-8code). If you've been following along in your style sheet, your Web page should look a lot better as well.

Some Simple JavaScript

JavaScript is the last part of building a Web page—the Web-page behavior. You add scripts to the head of your document similarly to how you add CSS. For example, if you have a script named `script.js`, you would add the following line in the <head> of your document to get it to run on your page:

```
<script type="text/javascript" src="script.js">
</script>
```

As with other technology on your page, always consider if you can do the same thing with items higher in the hierarchy before you turn to JavaScript or other client-side scripts. For example, one of the most popular uses for JavaScript is an image rollover—an image that changes when you put your mouse over it. The About.com JavaScript site explains how to do this with JavaScript (http://about.com/javascript/mouseover), but this is something that can now be done with CSS and HTML manipulations.

If you're interested in adding some JavaScript to your page as it is right now, then check out the About.com JavaScript script library (http://about.com/javascript/scriptlibrary) for ideas. On my site, I am going to leave out the JavaScript for now. In Chapter 7 we'll go into more detail about how to use JavaScript to good effect on a Web page. And then in Chapter 14 you'll find out some of the exciting places we can go with JavaScript.

TOOLS YOU NEED

▶ This was a crash course in cascading style sheets, but luckily it is possible to learn CSS more leisurely. On my site, I offer a free five-day course in CSS (http://about .com/webdesign/csscourse). After you finish the course, the CSS we went through above will seem like nothing. And if you want to go faster than five days, you can always request each lesson as soon as you finish the last one (http://about.com/webdesign/ csscoursefast).

Get Linked

The following links will help you to understand more about the HTML and CSS code that you'll be using to build your Web site.

STILL COMPLETELY LOST?

Do not fear. Even if you still don't think you can learn HTML or understand how to do Web design, I can help. This five-page guide takes you through building a Web page in baby steps. You can do it.

http://about.com/webdesign/stilllost

LEARN HTML

There are so many resources online for learning HTML, it's hard to know where to start. I've collected my beginning HTML resources into one location so that you can learn HTML at the pace that works for you.

http://about.com/webdesign/learnhtml

WHERE TO START WITH CSS

Cascading style sheets are very complicated, but the resources listed on this site will help you learn CSS and understand what we've covered in the book.

http://about.com/webdesign/startcss

Chapter 5

Creating a Content or Article Page

Why Start Here, and Not the Home Page?

Most designers, when they start to build a Web site, start with the home page and work down through the site. The problem is, the home page is very complicated and can involve people at every level of your company. You can find all the plans you made in Chapters 1 and 2 go out the window as the home page "evolves." The problem is, if you don't know what other pages are going to be on your site, it's hard to know what your home page should have on it.

Here's an example. On one job I worked on, we were asked to redesign the site's home page. Marketing had an opinion about what we should have on the page, as did sales, support, our VP, and the CEO. By the time we were done, the home page was required to link to about thirty different sections. We got the

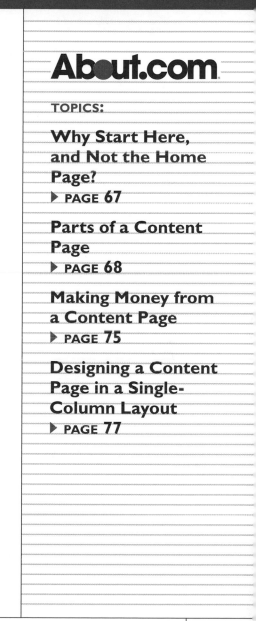

design approved and then went to marketing, sales, support, and our VP and asked for the content to build out their site sections. In each case we got a blank stare and then, "Well, I guess we don't need to have that site section on the home page for launch. We'll put it up once we have content for it." The home page went live with five or six site sections rather than the thirty we originally designed. Since then, I get the content of the Web site done before building the home page.

Content pages are the basis of information-focused Web sites. If your site will focus on providing information for your customers, you will need a lot of content pages to provide it. My About.com site is primarily an information-focused site, and after ten years, I have hundreds of articles and information for my readers.

Before you get worried that you'll need to provide that depth of information all at once, remember that I didn't create 1,000 articles overnight. When I opened my site, I had about ten articles live and a lot of links to other sites with other articles.

The best way to move forward with an information site is to start small and grow. There will always be more that you could be writing about; after nine years, my file of article ideas still grows faster than I can write the articles. The key is to release your site with a few articles (five to ten) and then set up a schedule to add more. My original schedule was one new article every one to two weeks.

Parts of a Content Page

There are three basic parts of a content page: the content, the navigation, and the advertisements and promotions. All are important if your site is going to be successful in providing the information your customers want and the revenue your business needs.

▶ The important part of an information site is the information. If you only have ten articles on your site, eventually people will have read them all and not need to come back. Sometimes, even with my file of ideas, I can't get inspired to write. When that happens I fall back on storyboarding to find inspiration. My article "What to Write About" (http://about.com/webdesign/contentideas) discusses how to storyboard Web project ideas.

The content is the most important part of a content page. Your CEO or sales department might argue that the advertising and promotions are more important to the company, but ultimately, if the customer isn't finding the information she is looking for on the content page, the ads are superfluous. And because content is the most important part of a content page, you need to pay attention to both how it is displayed on the page and the actual quality of the content.

There are two types of content that most Web pages provide: written content and visual content. Written content is what most people think of when they think of an information page, but information on Web pages can be effectively displayed through images. Photo galleries and visual how-to files are just two ways that you can provide information with photos rather than text.

Writing for the Web is different from offline writing. This is the first thing that most Web writers struggle to understand. But it's very important to remember. Just because you've written marketing briefs or white papers or even articles and fiction doesn't guarantee that your writing will be well received on the Web. There are some rules that to be aware of when writing for the Web:

- **Keep it short.** Web pages are hard to read because monitor quality and resolution still aren't up to paper standards. Shorter articles are easier on the eyes than long rambling ones.
- **Think in terms of lists.** Lists are easier to read online than paragraphs of text because the bullets or numbers call out the new sections and visually segment the text. If you add explanatory text below your list items, then call out the headlines in bold or another color.

ELSEWHERE ON THE WEB

▶ Beyond the rules of writing for Web pages, there are guidelines for writing interesting Web pages. The article "Ten Tips on Writing the Living Web" (http://alistapart. com/articles/writeliving) is one of my favorites. It focuses on writing more changeable pages such as weblogs, but the tips are great for putting some punch in your topic.

- **Use active verbs.** Keep the pace up with action words and tell your readers what to do. Avoid the passive voice except where it's absolutely required.
- **Subdivide your text.** HTML includes six levels of headings for a reason. Adding visual hierarchy to your Web pages makes them easier to scan and find the relevant information.
- **Link the text in your paragraphs.** Links are another visual cue that something is important. When you link the actual text inside a paragraph, rather than creating a list of links somewhere else on the page, it pulls your reader back onto the page they're reading and makes the paragraph easier to skim.
- **Don't link every word.** As with everything, moderation is the key. Choose the words you're linking to carefully, as carefully as you choose where you're going to link.
- **Link to things your readers want.** When your readers see a link on your page, they will think that it's important. If it's interesting enough, they will click on it. Ending up on a glossary page when they thought they were getting another article can be a huge letdown.
- **If you do nothing else, proofread your pages.** Web readers might not be more critical than magazine and book readers, but they are much quicker to send off a snippy e-mail pointing out your errors. It's simpler to avoid the errors as much as possible in the first place. When you do get a snippy e-mail pointing out an error, simply fix the error rather than being snippy in response.

Let's talk about links. Links are how people get around on your Web page, but they are also how they find information about your Web page—what's important, what information you provide, and what might be missing.

Web designers believe that customers coming to Web pages start at the top and read through from left to right down to the bottom of the page. But this isn't true. Most people coming to a Web page scan the page and bounce around. They see small snippets of the page content and then finally land on something that interests them and click away. You can see a visual representation of this in Steve Krug's excellent book *Don't Make Me Think* or in the chapter online (**www.sensible.com/chapter.html**).

Headlines and links are what your customers see when they are scanning through your page, looking for the information they need. Links stand out more than headlines because they imply some interactivity and are usually in a different color than the surrounding text. So creating effective links is vital to create content that your readers will find useful. The following rules will help you make your links useful:

- **Don't create a link that reads "Click Here."** "Click here" has absolutely no meaning in the context of your text. A better link gives your readers an idea of what they're going to get when they click or matches the headline of the resulting page.
- **Keep your links informative.** In the spirit of avoiding "click here," you want to have links that provide information.
- **Write links inline in the content.** Links that are found within the text of a document feel more authentic to people than lists of links.
- **Don't explain your links.** When you write a link that says something like "Go to this page to buy dog toys" you are calling attention to the mechanics of the Web page—in other words, that that text is a link. The simple fact that the text is typically in a different color and underlined should do that for you. A better link would read "Buy dog toys." It's

informative and gives the customer an idea of what they're going to get.

But there's more than just written content. Photos and pictures are also useful forms of Web content. Whether you are focusing on the images as the sole content for your page, as in a photo gallery, or as an addition to the written content on the page, images are vital to make a Web page interesting. But it is easy to make images that detract from your Web site.

Small images are good Web images. I can't stress this enough. Large Web images make your Web pages large, download more slowly, and look bad. There are a few things you can do to make your images smaller for Web pages:

- **Crop your images.** Make sure that the image contains only the relevant information. That doesn't mean you need to get so tight that it's hard to tell what you're looking at, but get rid of the extra stuff.
- **Check the resolution.** While this won't change the download size, you don't need your image to be 300 dpi if it's displayed on a Web page. Resolutions of 72 dpi or 96 dpi are fine and will discourage people from stealing your photos to print.
- **Use the right format for your image.** Photographs are best saved as **JPEG** files, while flat color images, like clip art, are best saved as GIF. If you're not sure, use your editing software to change the format and compare the resulting file sizes.
- **Don't use more colors than you need on GIF images.** With GIF images, you can index the file to use only the number of colors that are in the image. This will improve the file size

WHAT'S HOT

▶ Because links provide information about your Web page, creating links that help provide that information will improve your Web site. The key is to understand how readers use information Web sites and then tailor the links to match that. My article "Creating Better Links" (http://about.com/webdesign/betterlinks) can help.

without affecting the quality—if your image isn't using the color red, then it doesn't need red in its palette.

- **Use a high-quality image-editing tool**, like Photoshop or Paint Shop Pro. These tools will allow you to make more changes to your image size without affecting the quality.

Only use images where you need images. This concept is especially important on content pages. Images for things like drop caps, quotations, and call-outs may look fancy and nice, but they only increase the download time of your Web page. Search engines can't read the text written in images, so you lose the value of that text when optimizing for search. Plus, if your readers have images turned off or can't view images, they won't see the text. If that text is especially important to the content, it can make the page unreadable. Graphical drop caps can also make your page appear to have spelling errors. Even if you use alt text, search engines and screen readers won't recognize the image as part of the following text.

The second most important part of a content page is the navigation. Again, your marketing or sales departments might disagree, but navigation is the way that people get around your Web site, and on a content site that is funded by advertising, you want your pages to be seen. I will go into detail on how to build great navigation structures in Chapter 8, but here are some tips:

- **Keep your navigation simple.** If it's easy to understand, people will use it. If people are using the search function more than navigating on your site, then chances are the navigation is too hard.
- **Keep your navigation consistent.** You will find that some designers now advocate context-sensitive navigation, or

navigation that changes depending upon where you are. Inconsistent navigation confuses people.

- **Test your navigation ideas.** Keep what is working on your site, but don't be afraid to change what isn't working. When you test, you may find that context-sensitive navigation works well for your site or that complex navigation is better, regardless of what I've said.

And then there are the advertisements. Finding a place for advertisements on your content pages can be very important if your Web site is going to make money. It's important to remember that ads should not be the main focus on a customer-focused Web site. People aren't coming to your Web page for the advertisements; they're coming for the content.

This is a complaint about the way the About.com Web Design/HTML site is designed. I am not the About.com designer, so I can't say why it's designed as it is, but advertising is very important to the continued existence of About.com, and the Web sites reflect it. On my site, content pages only have around three or four advertisements above the fold, and only two are particularly close to the content of the page.

Most content Web pages place ads in the following locations:

- A banner ad across the top of the screen
- Small square ads in the left column above or below navigation
- Tower ads in the right column
- Large square ads intermingled with the content
- Pop-up and interstitial ads that appear when the page is loaded

TOOLS YOU NEED

▸ Understanding your customers is important for good navigation. If you use terms in your navigation that your customers don't understand, they won't be able to get around your site. Designing navigation that works is an art more than a science. If you want more help now, you can read my article "Navigating Web Pages" (http://about.com/webdesign/navigation).

When you are planning the page design and layout for a content page, you want to make sure that you have space allocated for advertising.

Making Money from a Content Page

Most content pages make their money from advertising. But there are several ways to make money from a content page:

- Donations
- Subscriptions
- Affiliate programs
- Related text ads
- Standard banner ads

Donations may seem like an unlikely way to make money from a Web page, but it is possible. There are many blog sites that have a PayPal donations link on their site to collect some extra cash. It may seem like begging, but a donation to keep an interesting Web site running isn't much different from paying to use a piece of shareware software.

Subscriptions are another way to make money from your Web content. The challenge here is that you need to make sure that you are providing content that people want and are willing to pay for. Many news sites capitalize on the subscription model by providing current articles for free but making access to their back issues available for pay, typically by subscription.

In order to set up a subscription site, you need to have content that people want to buy or that is hard to find in another source. A subscription model is hard for a small business just starting an information-focused Web site, but if your customers want your content, this might be a great way to make money. Another way subscriptions work is when there is an associated offline source that the Web-site subscription enhances. You see this with many magazines that offer an online version only to paying subscribers.

Affiliate programs are a very popular way to make money with content pages. There are many types of affiliate programs, from systems where you link to other Web sites to programs where you link to products for sale.

The most successful affiliate links are ones that are built into the context of your Web site. On my sample dog-toys Web site, the most successful affiliate programs I could set up would be ones that sold dog products or offered assistance to dog owners. Using Commission Junction (www.cj.com), I could set up affiliate links to Petco.com and PetCareRX.

Targeted text ads are a great way to get more money from your Web site. Text ads that match the content focus on a page do a lot better than less-targeted banner and visual ads. This is because the content in the text ad relates to the content on the page. For example, on my dog-toys site, I might have an article on dog leashes. If I have signed up for targeted text ads to be displayed on that site, my writing would focus on keywords like "dogs, leashes, dog toys," and I would get ads that are related to those same keywords.

Standard banner ads are the most recognizable source of income for content Web sites. The best way to add a banner advertising campaign is to join an affiliate program like LinkShare (www.linkshare.com) that offers banner advertising. Otherwise, small Web sites that are starting out don't have the number of page views that advertisers are looking for.

ELSEWHERE ON THE WEB

▶ Making money on the Web isn't a case of putting up a Web page and letting the cash roll in. You have to make an effort. Luckily there are other Guides on About.com who explain how. The Online Business Guide shows how to make money with affiliate programs (http://about.com/onlinebusiness/affiliateprograms) and the Entrepreneurs Guide takes a look at being an Amazon.com affiliate (http://about.com/entrepreneurs/amazonaffiliate).

Designing a Content Page in a Single-Column Layout

Now that we know the parts of a good content page, it's time to build one. First, set up your local copy of your Web site so that you can add content pages. Go back to your plan to determine how you want your directories to be structured. I am going to build a wide and shallow site, and one directory called "articles" will house all my articles.

I want to make sure that my local hard-drive file and folder names exactly match the file and folder names I will have on my site. That way, I can upload them all as one batch, without having to rename anything. I will be creating my new pages inside the articles directory, using the naming convention I came up with in Chapter 2.

Your content pages should all look roughly the same. This may seem boring or unoriginal, but content, not design, is the point of a content page. A well-designed page does not call attention to the design, but rather facilitates the customer's need to get information from that page.

Well-known Web designer and author Robin Williams wrote that a good design feature of a Web site is that "every Web page in the site looks like it belongs to the same site" (**www.ratz .com/featuresgood.html**). And Jakob Nielsen, a preeminent Web usability expert, says, "Consistency is one of the most powerful usability principles: when things always behave the same, users don't have to worry about what will happen" (**www.useit.com/ alertbox/9605.html**).

Here are the steps to start editing your new content page:

1. Create a new directory on your hard drive for your Web site. This will be the root of your Web site on your hard drive, so name it something you'll remember. This is the only directory

ELSEWHERE ON THE WEB

▶ One of the hottest targeted ads sites is Google AdSense (**https://www .google.com/adsense**). With AdSense, you have the power of Google behind your Web site—so you get a strong keyword analysis engine for your Web site. And while Google advertising looks the same on most sites, you can customize it to make it fit better with the style of your Web site.

that won't be mirrored exactly as it's named on your Web host, because on your Web host this directory will be your domain name.

2. Change to your new site directory and create an articles directory.
3. Open your Web editor.
4. Start a new Web page in the articles directory. Name it following your naming convention for your Web site. I'm going to write an article about dog leashes, and I'll name the file `dogleashes.html`.

All our pages will use CSS for layout. If you've built any Web pages in the last five to ten years, you may be comfortable doing all your Web page layout in tables, but that is not good form, and in fact is invalid XHTML. One commenter on my site said, "Tables ARE positioning elements!! Get over it." But this is incorrect. Tables in HTML are for tabular data, not for positioning content on the page. The rest of this book will discuss different layouts you can use for your Web pages and all of them will be done with cascading style sheets, not tables.

Let's start editing the article. As with our first page, you want to create a page that has your HTML and content on it. Because we know we're working on an article page, it's less important that we have the actual content that's going to be on the page, so placeholder text is all right. I'm going to use text referred to as "lorem ipsum"—Latin text that will allow us to look at the design rather than the words. You can get a copy of the text on the About.com Desktop Publishing site (http://about.com/desktoppub/loremipsum). Using placeholder text like this is called greeking.

For initial page designs, greeking is perfectly acceptable. Keep in mind, however, that in many cases it's not a good idea. In my article "Use Real Text for Testing Page Designs" (**http://about .com/webdesign/userealtext**), I explain some of the problems with designing a page without using real text.

For our content page we are going to create a page with many of the elements that we learned in Chapter 4. Before we worry about the layout, we need to get the site built. My HTML looks like this:

```
<!DOCTYPE html PUBLIC "-//W3C//DTD XHTML 1.0
Transitional//EN" "http://www.w3.org/TR/xhtml1/
DTD/xhtml1-transitional.dtd">
<html>
<head>
<title>Dog Leashes - Dogs and Their Toys</title>
<meta name="description" content="Dog leashes
restraint devices dog leashes" />
<meta name="keywords" content="dog leashes,
dogs, dog toys, canines, information about dogs,
dog help" />
</head>
<body>
<h1 id="branding">Dogs and Their Toys</h1>
<ul id="navigation">
<li><a href="../index.html">Home</a></li>
<li><a href="../products/index.html">Dog Toys
for Sale</a></li>
<li><a href="../articles/index.html">Dog Infor-
mation</a></li>
<li><a href="../about/index.html">About This
Site</a></li>
</ul>
<div id="body">
<h2>Dog Leashes</h2>
<p>Lorem ipsum dolor sit amet, consectetuer
adipiscing elit, sed diam nonummy. </p>
<p>Ut wisi enim ad minim veniam, quis nostrud
exerci tation ullamcorper suscipit. </p>
<h3>My Favorite Leashes</h3>
<ol>
<li>Ut wisi enim ad minim veniam</li>
```

ASK YOUR GUIDE

Why is there such a big fuss about tables versus CSS? Is CSS hard?

▶ CSS for layout is a new way of thinking about Web-page layout, and because of that it can be hard to learn, especially if you're used to thinking in tables. Back in Chapter 1, I said that atti-tude counts for a lot in Web design, and that applies here too. CSS is interesting, fun, and challenging, but it isn't hard if you have the right attitude.

```
<li>quis nostrud exerci tation ullamcorper</li>
</ol>
<p>Duis autem vel eum iriure dolor in hendrerit
in vulputate velit esse molestie</p>
<h3>My Least Favorite Leashes</h3>
<ol>
<li>Ut wisi enim ad minim veniam</li>
<li>quis nostrud exerci tation ullamcorper</li>
</ol>
</div>
<div id="information">
<p>Copyright &copy; 2006 <a href="http://webde-
sign.about.com/mpremail.htm">Jennifer Kyrnin</
a></p>
</div>
</body>
</html>
```

Since the page doesn't have any styles on it, we're back to the plain-looking page. I added some links into my navigation, based on my site plan. Note: the links I added are not **full path** links but rather **relative path**. If your Web editor doesn't do this for you automatically, you can learn more about full (absolute) and relative path links on my Web site (**http://about.com/webdesign/abso luterelative**). I also removed the extra div tag around the branding headline. If we need it, I can add it back in. I'm going to add back in some of the simple styles we had on the first page (as shown at **http://about.com/webdesign/example5-2**).

```
html, body { margin: 0px 20px; }
html { background-color : #3c6; }
body {
      width : 600px;
      font: normal 1em Geneva, Arial, Helvetica;
      background-color:#fff;
      padding: 0px 5px 5px 5px;
}
#information { font-size: .8em; }[EC]
```

The page would work for a basic site, but we need something else.

Figure 5-1: A basic article page

Dressing up the branding and headline would be a great start toward fixing this page. Since this is going to be my branding for the entire site, I need to create something that represents the site. I decided to use a photo of my dogs; this site is for them, after all.

This original photo was around 2200 × 1700 pixels in size and 11MB to download, huge for a Web page. I cropped it to get rid of extraneous items and also needed to make it smaller. For height, 200 pixels was about the smallest I wanted to go. (Any smaller, and McKinley is just a black smudge.) Finally, because this was going to be part of my logo, I wanted to get rid of everything but the dogs. I used the tips on the About.com Graphics Software site to remove the background (**http://about.com/graphicssoft/removebackground**) using Photoshop. If you're interested, I've put a smaller (but still not optimized) version of the original and the branding image up on my site: **http://about.com/webdesign/example5-4**.

But having the image isn't enough. I also need to adjust the CSS so that the image is displayed and the text is more like a page headline and less like a chunk of black text. So I added some additional CSS to style the headline and changed the existing CSS to adjust the spacing on the page.

```
html, body { margin: 0px 20px; }
html { background-color : #3c6; }
body {
      width : 600px;
      font: normal 1em Geneva, Arial, Helvetica;
      background-color:#fff;
}
#information { font-size: .8em; }
#branding {
      height: 200px;
      background: #fff url(dogs _ and _ toys _ logo.
   jpg) no-repeat;
      margin: 0;
      padding: 0 0 0 100px;
      font-size: 3em;
      color: #3c6;
}
```

As you can see, CSS changes a lot as you're building a page. Test new features as you add them and make sure that everything else remains as you want it.

For my final version of this page, I created a simple navigation menu at the top of the page using the same color scheme (green and white). I also centered the page in the browser window and gave the interior text a bit more room.

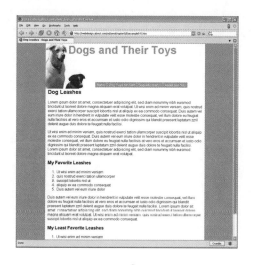

Figure 5-2: A nicer-
looking content
page

As you can see, the page is starting to shape up. If you've followed along with your site, then your page should be turning out nicely as well. This may be a fairly simple single-column layout, but it demonstrates some basics of CSS and how you can affect your pages.

Get Linked

Writing for a content-focused Web site can be a challenge. These links should help you write better content and generate more interesting content-focused Web sites.

WRITING FOR THE WEB

Beyond grammar and spelling, writing for the Web is very different from writing for print. These links will teach you how to write well for Web pages.

↗ http://about.com/webdesign/writing

LEARN MORE ABOUT CSS LAYOUTS

If you're still not sure why to build CSS layouts, the articles and information on this page can help explain it to you as well as how to do it.

↗ http://about.com/webdesign/csslayouts

Chapter 6

Creating a Product Page

How Is a Product Page Different from a Content Page?

The content pages we built in Chapter 5 had the primary goal of imparting information to readers. These pages would be things like articles and FAQs and information that your customers might be searching for on the Internet.

Product pages have a different goal. The goal of a product page is to sell something to someone. A product page can use information to help sell the product, but the information is not the goal of the page.

In a lot of ways, the success of a product page is a lot easier to judge. The only readily available metric for testing a content page is to count page views. The assumption is that if a content page gets a lot of page views, then it is providing information that people want. But since it's hard to tell how long people are staying on a page, it's hard to know if they read it or clicked "Back" immediately.

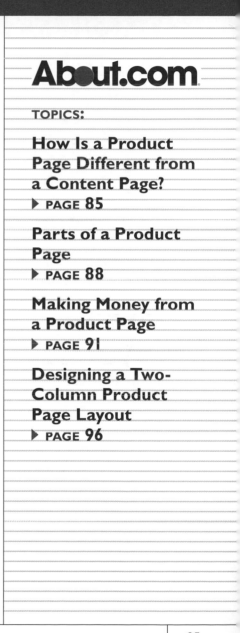

About.com

A product page also has the page-view metric, but more powerful and more measurable is the number of people who buy the product after they view a page.

Consider several things when you start designing a product page:

- **Know your customers.** What are their interests and how do they spend their time, online and offline? If there are popular forums or blogs that your customers frequent, then you should be there too, to find out what they are looking for. This can also help you to find new product lines and customers.
- **The style and look of your site should match your product and company.** It should also match your customers. For example, if you're selling extreme sports gear to a twenty-something male consumer, you want the style to be rough and edgy to match your customers' self-image as well as the other Web sites they frequent.
- **If you can, allow your customers to interact with the site.** This can be as simple as a feedback form or as complex as the Amazon.com system, with customer reviews and "People who bought this also bought" options. You can also have customer interaction by participating in forums that your customers use. Be sure to have real interactions and not just ads for your products.
- **Make sure that you're linking outside your site.** External links show your customers that you're willing to entertain outside opinions, and you're not afraid to let your product be seen and evaluated by the "sharks" that patrol the waters of the Internet.
- **Finally, make sure that your storefront or shopping cart functionality works well.** If you don't have a good and secure

way of selling your products, in the end all the other items don't matter.

There are problems with measuring page views. As I mentioned, without a very sophisticated (read expensive) log-analysis software program, it's hard to tell how long people spend on a Web page. This matters when it comes to content.

For example, I have a very popular two-page article on the SPAN and DIV tags (http://about.com/webdesign/spandiv). It regularly hits my most popular list (http://about.com/webdesign/most popular) without my promoting the article at all. The first page is around 500 words and would take the average person around five minutes to read on the Web. But because I only know how many views the page gets, I have no idea if anyone is sticking around to read it. I don't know if they skimmed for ten seconds and then left because it wasn't helpful or if they read the whole thing and then clicked on all the links looking for more information.

This makes it very difficult to gauge the success of a content page.

The focus of product pages is sales. You can track how many sales are generated from the Web product page. This is a huge time-saver when you're trying to improve your site to make it work better for your customers. If you make a change and sales go down, you know you should change it back. If you make a change and sales skyrocket, make sure that all your product pages use that new feature.

Tracking sales gives you a much more tangible result to follow versus just page views. You also know exactly how your efforts will affect the bottom line of your company. Some companies track every element of every Web page so they can tell exactly how much money each page, section, or even each link made.

ELSEWHERE ON THE WEB

▶ To sell products on the Web, you need a way to sell them. Granted, it's possible to use a simple order form or have your customers call you, but if you want to make real sales you need some type of e-commerce solution. The About.com Online Business Guide takes you through the steps of deciding if you need a shopping cart solution or an entire storefront (http://about.com/onlinebusiness/cartorstorefront).

If you study the source of a typical Amazon.com Web page, you will find codes on every link that indicate where on the page the link is. The link to a specific book might show up in two or three locations, and each link would be slightly different. That difference gives Amazon.com additional information, indicating whether you clicked on the link in the navigation column or somewhere else on the page.

This amount of analysis is beyond the scope of most small business Web sites, but it shows you the level of metrics you can aspire to. The more you measure, the more you can control and change. If you were Amazon.com and you knew that the third link in the first section of the page gets the most hits, you could place products there that need a boost in sales, while placing other, more sure sellers in less popular locations.

Parts of a Product Page

There are three basic parts to a product page: product information, navigation and branding, and content and advertising. The way those parts work together is a little different from a content page.

Because the primary focus of a product page is on selling something to your customers, you need to make sure that your navigation, branding, content, and advertising doesn't overwhelm the rest of the page. At one company I worked for, we made a lot of money through advertising on our content pages. But we also sold some products off the Web site. The decision was made early on that while we would have advertising on the content pages, any page that was devoted to selling product would not have advertising.

What are you trying to sell? That is your product information. The key to selling online is to provide enough information about your product that your customers want to buy but not so much that they get overwhelmed. The problem with this is that those two amounts of information can be very different.

The information section of your product page should contain the following elements:

- **Multiple ways to purchase:** This is the key to your product page. You need to make it as easy as you can to purchase your product. Since we're building a Web site, you'll definitely want a link to an online store or shopping cart, but good Web sites don't stop there. If you can, include information like sales phone numbers and brick-and-mortar store locations.
- **A photo of the product or service (if possible):** Pictures sell products much better than text. If your product is slick looking, a photo will tell me that, and I'll be more likely to want it.
- **A short descriptive paragraph or two about the product:** On the initial product page, you want to stay away from long marketing blurbs about how great your product is. Yes, be sure to market the product, but keep it short for the first page.
- **Links to more information:** Link to fact sheets, product brochures, downloadable PDFs, competitive information, or anything you have about the product.
- **Show how your product is received outside your company:** The easiest way to do this with a product page is to have links to reviews. If you don't have any reviews, have your PR team sending out review copies of your product and asking for reviews to link to. You also want to include any press mentions about your product on the page as well.
- **Provide opportunities for community collaboration:** One of the things that makes Amazon.com so successful is that

WHAT'S HOT

▶ More than where you place ads on your Web site, the style of those ads and how they are created can have a huge impact on both their effectiveness and how people perceive the pages they are on. My category on creating Web advertisements (http://about.com/webdesign/creatingads) is a valuable resource for anyone who wants to build ads or use them on their site.

I've heard that people scroll more now. Is getting things above the fold still so important?

▶ While it is true that customers scroll a lot more than they did five or ten years ago, it's still a good idea to get the important points in your content displaying near the top of the page. The challenge that most designers have is that there are so many definitions of what is important on a page. Each of the different departments in a company will have a different opinion on this. The best thing to remember is that you can't please everyone all the time. Build each page to be true to the goals of that page.

the customers can act as reviewers as well. If your product is suitable, you might want to link to a forum where people who use your product can chat about the product.

Navigation and branding need to be on your product pages. But you want to make sure that they don't take away from the product itself. On a content-focused site you might have a branding image that flows across the entire top of the page, similar to what we built in the last chapter (**http://about.com/web design/example5-6**). On a product site, your branding and navigation should take a smaller portion of the page.

Rather than devoting a large header row to your navigation and branding, you can use a simple logo and left navigation for the entire site, leaving the entire right column for your product information. This has the other advantage of getting the product content higher up on the page, or "above the fold."

On a product page, your navigation must reinforce what you have to offer the customer. If you have a lot of different types of products for sale, you want to have some indication of that in your navigation. That way, when a customer is on a product page, he knows that he is dealing with an entire company and not a one-hit wonder.

If you do only sell one product, you want your navigation to reflect your commitment to your customer. Your navigation should include elements like "Help" or "Support" so that your customers recognize you're going to stick around for a while. There is nothing more frustrating than buying something on the Internet and having the company go under right as you begin having problems with the product. If your site doesn't reassure your customers that you're in this business for the long term, you will have trouble wooing them away from established companies in the same industry.

Don't forget other content. While product pages have a focus on selling products, you will want other elements on these pages to keep them interesting. If you have a site that focuses on content as well as products, you might want to include links to related content on a product page. For example, if the page is selling a leash, you might want to link to related articles and also have your leashes linked on those article pages.

Many sites make money through advertising, even when products haven't been sold yet. If you have ads on a product page, make sure that they aren't the most prominent feature. Including them in a sidebar or at the bottom of the page is more effective than letting them steal the focus of the page by putting them above the fold. When designing your site, think about the design of each page type separately and make the decisions about content placement for each individually. Putting ads across the top of every page of your site might make sense to your advertising team, but not if they compete with sales of your actual products.

Making Money from a Product Page

It may seem obvious how you make money from a product page: You get people to buy the product you have for sale. But how do you do that?

The "Buy" link is the most important element on a product page. Marketing people call this the call to action. This is the part of the Web page that tells your customer what to do, and on a product page that will be to "buy now."

Just because it's the most important element doesn't mean that it should be in a giant font, bright red, bold, and blinking. You want your customers to know what to do when they get to the product page, and you also want them to want to do it.

Here are some things to think about when you're constructing the call to action for your product pages:

- **The "Buy now" link should be easy to find on the page.** It should be above the fold and close to the product image.
- **It should indicate where customers will be taken when they click.** For example, an "Add to cart" link implies that they will be adding the product to an online shopping cart, with the opportunity to continue shopping. A "Buy now" link could be taking them to an online store or an affiliate site, or it could be adding the item to a shopping cart.
- **Let your customers decide on as many of the details as possible up front.** For example, if you're selling software, providing a link to "Purchase a CD" and another to "Purchase download version" is a good idea. The shopping cart should automatically reflect their choice. If you can't pass the customer's information to the store, then don't request it. Nothing is more frustrating than having to enter information twice, and online customers get suspicious and lose trust in the site when this happens. When you lose their trust, you lose their business.
- **Finally, don't forget to state the price.** Prices shouldn't be a state secret, especially for consumer items. If you're running an auction, show the base price if you can't keep the current price live on the product page. If the price varies due to options, show the lowest price (with the least options) as your starting place, or show a range. Hiding the price does nothing but annoy customers.

Don't forget your product information pages. These pages provide additional information for customers who want to do more research. They should all have a photo of the product and a "Buy" link on them. Even if the page has a goal of providing additional content about the product, the goal of every product page is to sell the product.

It is always amazing to me how many companies forget about this. At one company I worked for, the sales team had to duplicate the marketing team's efforts and create a completely new version of all product pages to get a sales link included as a prominent part of each page. It took another three years for the sales team to get the all-important call to action added to all the FAQs, fact sheets, and system information pages.

Use community to your advantage. There are many ways you can do this when selling products. But you have to be careful. There is a strong aversion to spam or perceived spam on the Web, and if a community decides that you are there simply to advertise, you'll quickly become unwelcome.

If you're careful, there are some great ways to reinforce your brand and sell products through online communities:

- **Create a corporate blog.** These popular Weblogs are written by someone in the company. The best corporate blogs are written by someone who has an interesting writing style and valuable insight into the company or the products.
- **Participate in forums that are related to your product.** It can be very exciting for a forum member to realize that the question they asked on the "Modern Vespa Forum" was answered by someone who works for Vespa. It lends credibility both to the brand and to the company. But be very careful that you don't overdo it. Posting in external forums can end up seeming like one giant ad campaign, and that will ultimately backfire.

- **Comment on blogs that are related to your product.** As with forums, remember that you need to keep from seeming too much like an advertisement. Many blog software programs are now recognizing that posts that read something like "I agree. <URL>" or "Nice site. <URL>" are spam and will block them from being posted. Some companies have tried hiring people to post links in blog comments, but that is starting to backfire as well, as readers become more and more sophisticated. It's better to participate in the conversation and provide your URL as part of your comment login.

- **Provide a forum for your customers to chat.** This gives them an opportunity to solve problems among other users of your product, and it provides you with insight into what is causing problems for your customers. You also don't have to be as careful in a forum that your company hosts; your customers will expect you to promote your own products.

Affiliate shops are a great way to sell products online. The first online store I ever built was a bookstore that sold books through Amazon.com. Affiliate programs can be a great way to make money online. You don't need any of the e-commerce programming, servers, or back end to build and maintain them. You also don't need to store or ship any products—all of that is handled by the company you're affiliated with.

The key to making money through affiliate programs is to have content that draws people into your Web site and then products that are related to that content. The most obvious content would be reviews. If you're reviewing a product such as a video, CD, book, or computer part, having a link to buy the product only makes sense, especially if you give it a good review.

Some of the better affiliate programs include:

Amazon.com

Amazon.com is one of the oldest affiliate programs around, and it works well. The nice thing about being an Amazon.com associate is that you can sell so many different things.
http://affiliate-program.amazon.com/gp/associates/join

Commission Junction

Commission Junction (CJ) provides advertising and affiliate opportunities in hundreds of different categories. Chances are good that if you want to sell it, CJ has an affiliate program for it.
www.cj.com

LinkShare

LinkShare is a huge compendium of sites, not just links as its name implies. A lot of About.com Guides use LinkShare.
www.linkshare.com/affiliates/index.shtml

You can also set up a storefront. If you don't want to sell someone else's products, there are still a lot of options out there for setting up a storefront, even if you don't want to host your store yourself.

Many people have set up very lucrative eBay businesses. It's easy to set up an eBay store, and having a storefront there gives you more credibility than linking to auction listings. You can also set up a store on Amazon to sell your products. Using a shopping cart solution or store that is maintained by another company allows you to concentrate on selling your products without having to worry about security and online transactions.

Security is crucial in an online store. The quickest way to lose a customer online is to not have a secure Web site. At a minimum, that means that your shopping cart or online store must be on a secure (**SSL**) connection when your customers begin to enter any data into the site. You can tell if a Web site is secure because the Web browser will have some type of lock icon and the URL should start with "https" rather than "http." If you're hosting your own shopping cart, you'll need to invest in a secured server certificate for your Web server. Some hosting providers offer this as a part of the service; talk to your hosting provider for more information.

Also part of the security of your Web site is how you'll accept payment. Most online Web sites accept credit cards, which can be an additional expense to support. You can also set up your store to accept PayPal (**www.paypal.com**), which offers business accounts and the option of credit card processing.

Finally, when thinking about security on your site, always provide a privacy policy for your customers to read if they want to. Always tell your customers what you will do with the collected information. And if you want to be even more reassuring to your customers, get your privacy policy reviewed by TrustE (**www.truste.com**).

Designing a Two-Column Product Page Layout

Now that you know all the things you should and shouldn't have on a product page, let's build a page. Two columns on a Web page give you a bit more flexibility. We can do things like put navigation in one column and main content in the other. We could also put the product content in the main column while a blog or other subsidiary content lives in the second column. For this book, I'll show you how to create a two-column layout that you can then adapt to meet your site's needs.

Start with the HTML for your product page. It's tempting to create two divs, one for each column, but for this basic page, I'm going to use the navigation as one column, and the div for the other. Since my navigation is an unordered list, I don't need another div to surround it. I can style the list itself. The HTML for the page looks like this:

```
<!DOCTYPE html PUBLIC "-//W3C//DTD XHTML 1.0
Transitional//EN" "http://www.w3.org/TR/xhtml1/
DTD/xhtml1-transitional.dtd">
<html>
<head>
<title>Buy a Dog Leash - Dogs and Their Toys</
title>
<meta name="description" content="Dog leashes
restraint devices dog leashes" />
<meta name="keywords" content="dog leashes,
dogs, dog toys, canines, information about dogs,
dog help" />
</head>
<body>
<ul id="navigation">
<li><a href="../index.html">Home</a></li>
<li><a href="../products/index.html">Dog Toys
for Sale</a></li>
<li><a href="../articles/index.html">Dog Infor-
mation</a></li>
<li><a href="../about/index.html">About This
Site</a></li>
</ul>
<div id="body">
<h1 id="branding">Dogs and Their Toys</h1>
<h2>Buy a Dog Leash</h2>
<p>
Lorem ipsum dolor sit amet, consectetuer adipi-
scing elit, sed diam nonummy nibh.
</p>
<p>
Ut wisi enim ad minim veniam, quis nostrud
exerci tation ullamcorper suscipit.
</p>
<p id="information">
Copyright &copy; 2006 <a href="http://webdesign.
about.com/mpremail.htm">Jennifer Kyrnin</a>
</p>
</div>
</body>
</html>
```

I will use the float style **property** to create the two columns. The advantage to this is that I can change the location of the columns simply by changing the direction of the floats. See the samples online. Example 6-1 (**http://about.com/webdesign/example6-1code**) has the navigation in the left column, and Example 6-2 (**http://about.com/webdesign/example6-2code**) has it in the right.

The CSS for Example 6-1 looks like this:

```
html, body { margin: 0; padding: 0; }
#body { width: 800px; }
#navigation {
  width: 160px;
  float: left;
}
#main {
  float: right;
  width: 600px;
}
```

The CSS for Example 6-2 looks like this:

```
html, body { margin: 0; padding: 0; }
#body { width: 800px; }
#navigation {
  width: 160px;
  float: right;
}
#main {
  float: left;
  width: 600px;
}
```

But these pages don't have any of the features of a good product page. In Example 6-3, I've added a photo and some links to more information about the product as well as a button to purchase the product from my shopping cart. The "Add to Cart" button looks like an image, but I've used CSS styles to make it stand out on the page. You can see the HTML and CSS I used to achieve this online in Example 6-3 (**http://about.com/webdesign/example6-3code**)

Figure 6-1: Selling the product

Two columns give you a lot of leeway in placing things on the page. If you don't want to use your navigation as a column, you can change that to a separate div and put a blog, news links, related product links, or even short articles on the page in the columns with the navigation. Another idea is to create equal-sized columns. There are thousands of Web sites that use a narrow column for navigation or sidebar elements and a wide column for the main elements, but no rule says you have to do it that way. Changing the width of your columns can give your Web design some spice. Play with what you're doing; don't just copy my HTML and CSS onto your site.

Get Linked

Selling products online is a great way to increase your sales or start a new business, but there are lots of ways to do it and things to learn. These links will take you further in selling online products.

E-COMMERCE

These links will get you started building an online store front and help you with all the steps you need to sell products online.
http://about.com/webdesign/ecommerce

AFFILIATE PROGRAMS

Even if you don't have products of your own to sell, you can sell other products and make a profit—with affiliate programs.
http://about.com/webdesign/affiliateprograms

Chapter 7

Contact Us and Information Pages

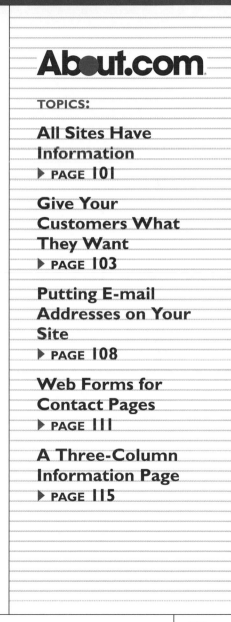

All Sites Have Information

Information pages on a Web site can be the most difficult to build because they tend to be a little bit of everything. Information pages are a lot like content pages in that they provide information. But because they are not the core of your Web site, information pages are often forgotten when designing a Web site.

Information pages are the pages on your Web site that are not content, products, navigation, or the home page. These are the pages that provide information about your company and/or yourself, how to contact you, or general information about your business.

If you're anything like me, you create your information pages once and then forget about them. But these pages matter. Information pages provide vital context to your customers. Contact pages allow your customers to provide feedback. And information pages reassure your customers that you are in it for the long haul, so they will trust what you provide.

Here are some examples of information pages on the About .com Web Design/HTML site:

My Biography Page

My biography hasn't changed that much on About.com, but it does provide information about me that might be useful to someone trying to decide if I know what I'm talking about when it comes to Web Design and HTML.
http://about.com/webdesign/biopage

Contact the Guide

This page is more than a contact page; before I show my e-mail address, I give information on where to get help and suggestions on how to find it.
http://about.com/webdesign/contactpage

Privacy Policy

This is another typical type of information page: legal documents required on most Web sites. I don't have any control over documents like these; they are posted and maintained by About.com.
http://about.com/webdesign/privacypolicy

Information pages are a lifeline for any site. They provide vital information to customers so that they can make informed decisions about you. But many companies make their information pages cute or overwhelming, and many companies omit information that customers want.

Give Your Customers What They Want

This is the key to any page on your Web site, but it's especially true of your information pages. These pages don't get very many page views on any given day, but taken in aggregate, they get a lot of views. And if you're not providing the information your customers want, they won't believe that you can provide the information they want on your core content and product pages, either.

On "Contact Us" pages, your customers want contact information. That might seem like an obvious thing, but you'd be surprised how many sites either don't provide that information or make it hard to find.

If your "Contact Us" page doesn't include the following information in an obvious location, rethink the page:

- **Support e-mail:** When your customers want to contact you, it's because they need support of some kind. Even if you don't have a support department, include an e-mail address or contact form for where to get support. Your customers would also appreciate a phone number for support, but if it's not toll-free, or they have to wait on hold a long time, they get testy.
- **Sales phone number:** You can also include an e-mail address, but your salespeople will want to talk to the customers directly. Keep in mind that if the phone number is toll-free, you'll be getting a lot of support calls on that line as well.
- **Webmaster e-mail:** Your customers want to report problems with your Web site when they come to a "Contact Us" page on the Web. If you don't provide a separate place for these comments to go, they'll all get sent to whatever address is on the page.

- **Storefront locations:** This isn't as important if your company is completely Web based. But it's always good to have some type of mailing address, even if it's a post office box. Some people feel more comfortable sending postal mail than e-mail.

"About Us" pages should include basic information about your company. Again, this seems like it should be obvious, but it's easy to get sidetracked and turn these into catch-alls. "About Us" pages should include information about the company rather than the site itself. A site map is a good idea if your Web site is larger than a few pages, but a site map is different than an "About Us" Web page.

Here are some of the more common elements of "About Us" pages:

- **At least one paragraph describing the company:** If you have a large number of things on your "About Us" page, then a paragraph is all you need. If you have less content, you can spend more time talking about your business age.
- **Links to your product or information categories:** This is especially important if your company's revenue is driven primarily from the Web site. You want to make sure your customers know what you offer.
- **Investor or shareholder information:** This is where investor information is found for publicly traded companies. Many sites include things like the current stock price or concise information from the latest financial statements. The "About IBM" page (**www.ibm.com/ibm/us**) demonstrates this well.
- **News and press information:** Some sites have a completely separate location for press releases, while others include the latest press releases on their home page. If your company

has press releases, you should provide a link to them on your "About Us" Web page.

- **Contact information or a link to the "Contact Us" page:** I like it when Web sites include their address, phone, and e-mail address on the "About Us" Web page because it means one less click if I decide I need to talk to them.

Make sure your legal pages are not intimidating. This is a challenge for pages like privacy policies, user agreements, copyright information pages, and other important legal pages you might want to have on your Web site. Usually you can't change the wording without taking it back to your lawyer, but there are things you can do to make sure they are useful to your customers without being overwhelming:

- **Mark up the pages with HTML and CSS.** When I started working at Symantec, one of the first jobs I was given was to maintain the legal notices page. Until then, the legal notices page had always been written by the legal department. The Web team would take that Word document and paste it into Dreamweaver to add paragraph tags and post it to the Web site. With all the all-caps sections and no segment headers or any styling, the page was impossible to read. Adding in styles helped our customers to understand what notices we were applying, and adding in navigation links also helped them get to the parts that were important to them.
- **Separate the different notices on different pages.** If someone is interested in your privacy policy, he is less interested in your copyright information or what patents you hold. If you only want to maintain one legal page, that's fine; but you should provide navigation on that page to the various sections so that your customers can see what you

offer right away without having to wade through the legal jargon.

Figure 7-1: Symantec legal notices with styles

● **Keep the pages up to date.** Your legal department may have all the latest versions of your legal notices, but that doesn't help your customers if they're not online.

I like to play "spot the copyright" around February of each year. You can play it in January, but I like to give sites a fair chance. The game is to go to sites and see if they've updated their copyright notice to the current year. It's true that if they haven't updated the site, they shouldn't change the year, but you'd be amazed how many sites have outdated copyright notices on brand-new content.

Legal pages are an important part of your Web site. They tell your readers that you are serious about your content and you will protect your rights. You don't have to go into a lot of detail, but you should have at least these two legal notices on your site: a privacy policy, if you collect any information from your customers, and a copyright notice.

There are lots of other types of legal notices you might want to have, like a patent notices page, trademark information, and investor notifications. About.com also has an ethics policy that we use to define what you can expect from the Guides and our content, and we have a user agreement that defines the rules that we will enforce on any customer interacting on our site.

Employment available is an important information page. The jobs page or section of your Web site can be very complex or very simple. The best jobs pages indicate, first and foremost, the jobs that are available. While people looking for a job are interested in what packages you offer and whether you have day care or a health plan with dental, they are usually looking for work and want to know if you have a job that would suit them. Once they've found that job, then they'll want to know about benefits. Don't hide the available jobs on a second page. If you have jobs you desperately need to fill, put them at the very top of the page.

Make it easy for your potential applicants to apply for the job. There is nothing more frustrating for a hiring manager than to have a job available but no applicants. If you have an online Web form for applications, make sure that it works, and test it whenever you change it.

In one horrible debacle, my team and I inadvertently changed one of the form fields while making a minor change to a job application form. Our team tested to make sure that the form was sending the data, but the people in charge of the data didn't think to test to make sure it was arriving. We didn't find out until around a month later that no jobs were going into the database. We test every step of every process now!

Your press releases can be an important information source. Once your company gets big enough to send out regular

ASK YOUR GUIDE

I thought if I put something on the Web, that made it public domain, and not copyrightable. Is this true?

▶ Copyright on the Web seems to be a tricky thing for people. The act of putting your content on the Web does not make it part of the public domain. I can't tell you how many times I've found articles I've written posted on some other Web site. When I contact the owners, they almost always respond by saying they found the article on the Web. It's okay to link to someone else's Web content, but it's not all right to copy it. I've written an article on Web copyright to help explain this (http://about.com/webdesign/copyright).

press releases, you will want to post them online. If you're a publicly traded U.S. company, you are required to make them available to your shareholders. An information section for press releases and the press is a good idea. It should include the following:

- **Press releases:** If your press page is full of information, you can separate your releases out onto dated sub-pages. But if you only make a few press releases a year, you can link to all of them from your press page.
- **Press contacts:** You want members of the press to talk to your PR department. You can have this information on your "Contact Us" page, but that usually results in spam from customers looking for support from any source.
- **Press resources:** Resources for the press include anything from print-ready logos or photos of you or your products to fact sheets and brochures about your products or company. When I review products for my About.com Web Design/ HTML site, I find it very useful when the company includes product shots for the press to use right on the site.

Putting E-mail Addresses on Your Site

Contact pages are all about helping your customers get in contact with you, and one of the easiest ways for your customers to contact you is by e-mail. But the problem with e-mail is that you get more than contact with customers—you get contact with spammers.

It's easy to add an e-mail link on your Web site. These are called **mailto links** because that is the code you use to tell the browser the link is to e-mail. For example, if I wanted to build a link to my Web Design / HTML e-mail address on my site, I would write:

```
<a href="mailto:webdesign.guide@about.com">Send
mail to Jennifer Kyrnin, the Web Design/HTML
Guide</a>
```

Mailto links are just like regular anchor links that we learned about in Chapter 4. The only difference between them is that instead of a Web URL in the `href=""` section, you write `mailto: e-mail address`.

Using `mailto:webdesign.guide@about.com` will cause the browser to open an e-mail client new message window and then your customer can start typing the mail. But there's more you can do to customize the message.

If you want to define the subject of the message, you can add that to your mailto line: `href="mailto:webdesign.guide@ about.com?subject=Web Design Help"`. As you can see, all you need is a question mark after your e-mail address and then "subject=" with your subject following. When your customer clicks on the link, the subject will be filled in with your default message.

Avoiding spam and viruses is important, too. The drawback to putting up an e-mail address on your Web site is that you will eventually get spam from that link. There are many ways to protect your e-mail address from spam, starting with how you post your address on your Web page through spam blockers at your e-mail client.

Unfortunately, with the amount of spam that arrives these days, you'll want to use as many different spam-blocking tools as you can. Here are some that I use:

- **Use a Web form instead of a mailto link.** I use this method a lot when I have structured information I want to collect.

TOOLS YOU NEED

▶ You can also add things like cc, bcc, and additional to line e-mail addresses to your mailto links. I cover that in my article on mailto (http:// about.com/webdesign/mailto). Another interesting thing you can do with mailto is to use it to make your forms work (http://about.com/web design/forms). Be careful. Mailto forms don't work with every browser/e-mail client combination and can result in problems (http://about.com/ webdesign/formproblems).

▶ Spam may be annoying, but if you get a virus because your e-mail address is on your Web site you'll be more than annoyed. There are computer viruses that scan Web pages to find more e-mail addresses to target and spread the virus. And some malicious ones will also do things to disable your computer after they're done spreading. When I wrote "Don't Catch a Virus from Your Web Page" (http://about.com/webdesign/virus protection), some people seemed to think I was over-reacting, but with viruses like SirCam and others out there, it's important to protect yourself and your site.

For example, if you want to submit your site to the Web Design Gallery (http://about.com/webdesign/designgallery), you need to post specific items about the site. You could put up a mailto link, but people would almost certainly leave things out that you need. So you put up a form that sends you an e-mail (http://about.com/webdesign/gallerysubmit).

- **Add anti-spam messages to your e-mail address.** This is a great solution if you assume that the people writing to you are looking at the e-mail address before they hit send. Instead of putting in your actual e-mail address, you include some additional text that a human would recognize as not part of the address and remove, like `mailto:webdesign.guideNOSPAMDELETETHISPART@about.com`. The problem is that many people don't read the e-mail address before they hit send, and their message will bounce.

- **Turn your e-mail address into an image.** The only way to prevent spammers and robots from getting your e-mail address is to leave it out of the alt text. I don't like using images in this way because it makes the image inaccessible. (See Chapter 13 for more details on accessibility.)

- **Use a disposable e-mail address** (http://about.com/email/disposableemail). You can weed out the spammers more quickly and make sure that legitimate customers get your real address once they need it.

- **Get a good spam-fighting program.** There are many available, and most deal with spam as it arrives in your mailbox. The About.com E-mail Guide recommends that you get one that removes the spam before you ever download it to your mailbox (http://about.com/email/antispam).

Web Forms for Contact Pages

It may seem like the safest thing to do is to use a contact form on your Web site and avoid all the problems that mailto links can cause. But there are as many issues with using Web forms for "Contact Us" pages as there are benefits.

There are many benefits to using Web forms for contact pages. Aside from avoiding spam and viruses, Web forms make your contact pages look more professional.

Web forms also encourage your customers to provide you with useful information. One e-mail exchange I had with a customer went on for three days. He sent in his question, and I responded asking him for a URL so I could see the page he was having trouble with. He responded with more information about the question, but no URL. We went back and forth like that for some time. If I'd had a Web form, I could have made URL a required field.

Be aware of the drawbacks to Web forms. One of the biggest is that forms are hard to build and maintain. Beyond a form page built in HTML, you need some type of program to run when the submit button is clicked. If your hosting provider doesn't have a form-to-e-mail script, you must get one for your site.

Did you think that forms might protect you against spam? Well, not anymore. Many spammers specialize in spamming forms automatically.

Let's build a Web contact form. The first thing you'll need to do is create a page for the form. For now, let's create a basic Web page with the <html>, <head>, and <body> tags. (We don't care about styles for the moment.)

ASK YOUR GUIDE

But what about mailto forms?

▶ No script is needed to make a form send e-mail. You can use a mailto command in the form `action` attribute that acts similarly to mailto in an anchor link. But there is more to it than that (http://about.com/web design/htmlformstutorial). Plus, mailto forms don't always work as you intend them to and can cause more frustration. But if you're willing to work through those issues you can use mailto as your form action for "Contact Us" forms.

The first tag you need for a form is, not surprisingly, `<form>` . . . `</form>`. The form tag takes several attributes, and we care about three of them:

`action`
This is the command that will run when the form is activated. Forms are usually activated by clicking on a submit button. For this example we'll create a mailto form, so the action will have mailto:e-mailaddress in it.

`method`
This tells the browser how to send the data. Your choices are GET or POST. Because we're creating a mailto form, the best method to use is GET. Some browsers have trouble with POST in a mailto form.

`enctype`
The enctype attribute tells the browser how to encode the data that is sent. Always encode mailto data as "text/plain" so that no unexpected codes get added.

The HTML for our form page should look something like this:

```
<!DOCTYPE html PUBLIC "-//W3C//DTD XHTML 1.0 Tran-
sitional//EN" "http://www.w3.org/TR/xhtml1/DTD/xhtml1-
transitional.dtd">
<html>
<head>
    <title>Contact Dogs and Their Toys</title>
    <meta name="description" content="Send your
question to the Dogs and Their Toys team. " />
    <meta name="keywords" content="dogs, dog toys,
canines, information about dogs, dog help, contact us" />
</head>
<body>
<h1>Dogs and Their Toys</h1>
<h2>Contact Us</h2>
```

```
<form action="mailto:webdesign.guide@about.com"
method="get" enctype="text/plain">
</form>
</body>
</html>
```

You can see the HTML for this form online at **http://about.com/ webdesign/example7-1code**.

There is nothing in the form, so the only thing that will show up on the page is the headline and subhead. For the rest of the HTML examples, I will assume that you know to leave in the basic HTML elements like <html>, <head>, and <body>, so I'll only display the form HTML.

The next step is to populate the form. Since this is a contact form, we'll want to ask for information like the customer's name, e-mail address, if he wants a reply, and what his message is. For this we'll use a bunch of different form tags (**http://about.com/web-design/formtags**). One of the tags I'll use that you might not be familiar with is the <label> tag. This tag helps make your forms more accessible. I have written an article about it on my About .com site (**http://about.com/webdesign/labeltag**).

First I'll ask for the person's name. For simplicity I'll make one form field for the full name. The e-mail address is a text field just like the name, so I'll write that now too (see online Example 7-2, **http://about.com/webdesign/example7-2code**).

```
<form action="mailto:webdesign.guide@about.com"
<mailto:webdesign.guide@about.com%C2%B2>
<mailto:webdesign.guide@about.com&#8221;>
<mailto:webdesign.guide@about.com%E2%80%9D>
method="get" enctype="text/plain">
<label accesskey="n" for="name">Name:
<input type="text" name="name" id="name"
value="" size="40" /></label><br />
<label accesskey="e" for="email">Email:
<input type="text" name="email" id="email"
value="" size="40" /></label></form>
```

Asking for a reply is a yes-or-no question, so rather than a text field I'll use a radio button. For the message field, I want the customer to be able to write as much as she needs to, so I'll make that a textarea. (See online Example 7-3, **http://about.com/webde sign/example7-3code.**)

```
<form action="mailto:webdesign.guide@about.com"
method="get" enctype="text/plain">
<label accesskey="n" for="name">Name: <input
type="text" name="name" id="name" value=""
size="40" /></label><br />
<label accesskey="e" for="email">Email: <input
type="text" name="email" id="email" value=""
size="40" /></label><br />
Do you want a reply?
<label accesskey="y"><input type="radio"
name="reply" id="reply" value="yes" /> Yes</
label>
<label accesskey="n"><input type="radio"
name="reply" id="reply" value="no" /> No</
label><br />
What is your message?<br />
<textarea name="message" id="message" rows="10"
cols="35"></textarea>
</form>
```

The only thing missing from our form now is a way to sub-mit the data. It's also nice to include a reset button, in case the customer wants to clear the form to write a new message. (See online Example 7-4, **http://about.com/webdesign/example7-4code**.)

```
<form action="mailto:webdesign.guide@about.com"
method="get" enctype="text/plain">
<label accesskey="n" for="name">Name:
<input type="text" name="name" id="name"
value="" size="40" /></label><br />
<label accesskey="e" for="email">Email:
<input type="text" name="email" id="email"
value="" size="40" /></label><br />
```

```
Do you want a reply?
<label accesskey="y"><input type="radio"
name="reply" id="reply" value="yes" /> Yes</
label>
<label accesskey="n"><input type="radio"
name="reply" id="reply" value="no" /> No</
label><br />
What is your message?<br />
<textarea name="message" id="message" rows="10"
cols="35"></textarea><br />
<input type="submit" value="Send Message" />
<input type="reset" value="Clear Form" />
</form>
```

Once you have the form written, you can change the e-mail address to your own e-mail address and test it out. Upload the page to your site and fill in the form details. Your browser should use the associated e-mail client to send the form data.

A Three-Column Information Page

Information pages typically need to have more content than a standard page. Having additional columns can help you get more information higher on the page than with a different layout.

To build a three-column layout, you first create a two-column layout then nest two more columns inside one of the columns. As we learned in Chapter 6, a two-column layout is easy to build.

If we take our "Contact Us" page from Example 7-4 and add in some div tags and a style sheet, we can start to build our layout. I've added a div before my main body and a div surrounding the main body and given them both ids (see online Example 7-5, **http://about.com/webdesign/example7-5code**).

```
<body>
<div id="subcol"></div>
<div id="maincol">
<h1>Dogs and Their Toys</h1>
```

```
<h2>Contact Us</h2>
<form action="mailto:webdesign.guide@about.com"
method="get" enctype="text/plain">
. . .
</form>
</div>
</body>
```

But having the divs in the document doesn't do anything for the design, so I added some content in the left column and left the "Contact Us" form in the middle. Since this is a three-column layout in Example 7-6, I have added three more divs: one will hold the entire site called "whole." (I would put the width on the body property itself, but IE 6 doesn't like that, so I'm adding another div.) One will hold the right column information, and one last div will hold the form in the middle. You can view the HTML online (Example 7-6: **http://about.com/webdesign/example7-6code**). The CSS to build this with two columns looks like this:

```
html, body { margin: 0px; }
html { background-color : #fff; }
body { font: normal 1em Geneva, Arial,
Helvetica; }
#whole { width: 800px; }
#subcol { float: left; width: 180px; }
#maincol { float: right; width: 610px; }
```

The last step to getting the design to work correctly is to add content into the outer column and test in my browsers to make sure it looks all right. I added some CSS to make the two inner columns align correctly, plus some extra styles to put borders around the columns so you could see them better. The HTML is online (Example 7-7: **http://about.com/webdesign/example7-7code**) and the CSS looks like this:

```
html, body { margin: 0px; }
html { background-color : #fff; }
body { font: normal 1em Geneva, Arial,
Helvetica; }
#whole { width: 800px; }
#subcol { float: left; width: 180px; border:
solid 1px red; }
#maincol { float: right; width: 610px; border:
dotted 1px red; }
#innercol { float: left; width: 400px; border:
solid 1px blue; }
#outercol { float: right; width: 200px; border:
dashed 1px blue; }
```

Now that I have the basic layout, I can start playing with the design. I'll put the list on the right side, and I should add some basic site navigation into the page so that my customers can get around.

Figure 7-2: The final design of a "Contact Us" page

You can see the HTML and CSS of my final design online (Example 7-8, http://about.com/webdesign/example7-8code). If both outside columns are used for content, there unfortunately isn't a lot of room for navigation. But there is a lot of room in the columns to add navigation in various locations.

Get Linked

Information pages can be challenging to write, but the following sites on my About.com Web Design/HTML site will help you get what you need.

HTML FORMS

HTML forms are an advanced HTML skill because you need to do more than build the Web page and styles. You also need to build how the form will behave. These articles will help you learn how to do both sides.

http://about.com/webdesign/htmlforms

FREE CGIS

The easiest way to add a form to your Web site is to use a free CGI to populate it. The CGIs listed here are not all form to e-mail, but they all give you useful things to add to your Web site.

http://about.com/webdesign/cgiscripts

LEGAL ISSUES

When building a Web site, there are always legal issues you need to deal with. Copyright is just the beginning.

http://about.com/webdesign/legal

AUTOMATE YOUR PRIVACY POLICY

You can write your privacy policy in XML and have it automatically checked and verified. There are even sites that will validate that you are following your privacy policy once you put it online in this format.

http://about.com/webdesign/p3p

Chapter 8

Navigating Your Site

Review Your Site Plan

When I first began designing pages, I built a site with ten to fifteen items in the navigation. Each navigation element consisted of one page, with no sub-pages. I felt that this made the site easier to understand, and in some ways I was right. After all, every page on the site was included in the navigation. Then I started testing it with my customers. What I determined through testing was that because I had so many things in the navigation menu, people thought the site was much larger than it was. They would click on an item in the navigation, and then start skimming that page. When I asked them what they were thinking, they'd say something like "Where is the rest?"

Navigation talks to your customers. Eye-tracking tests have found that Web-site readers tend to ignore elements at the very top and on the left and right sides of the page, all common locations for navigation and advertising. Instead, readers focus on the middle third of the page, where content is usually found. But just

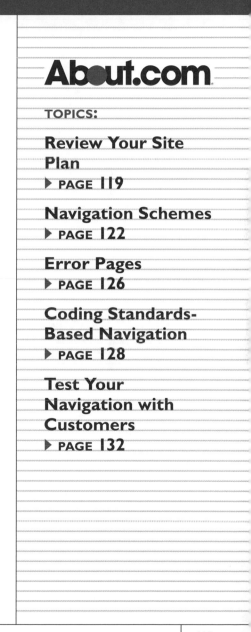

because they aren't looking at it doesn't mean they don't know the navigation is there.

Navigation acts as a security blanket for your customers. It is a comfortable region around the edges of the page that tells them they will find what they're looking for. Three types of navigation can be found on Web pages:

- **Access points:** These are elements of the navigation that take your customer somewhere else. This is what most people think of when they think of navigation—the menu at the top or on the left that takes readers to a new place on the site. Access points on my About.com site include the Essentials and Topics listed on the left side of every page, page links on the right side of articles, and additional related articles at the bottom of every article.
- **Signposts:** These are the elements on the page that tell your readers where they are in the site. This can be as simple as a headline or subhead that matches the title of the page in the title bar. Or they can be complex **breadcrumb trails** that follow your readers through the site as they click links. On my About.com site, signposts include the breadcrumb trail at the top, the page title and site title above every article, and the About.com logo.
- **Maps:** Maps are overviews of the site that help your customers find things. These include elements like site maps and category listings. On my About.com site, I have a site map, category listings for the topics I cover, lists of articles I've written, and more. I have over 5,000 pages on the site, so I need a lot of maps to keep it straight.

Navigation shouldn't be complicated. The best Web sites have fairly simple navigation. This can be a challenge to build especially if your site offers a little bit of everything. Take 3M, for example. They make nearly everything you can imagine, but their primary access points consist of five elements: "Products & Services," "Brands," "Technologies," "Our Company," and "Partners & Suppliers" (http://solutions.3m.com/en_US). Each of those access points takes you to a map page with a lot more information and links, but the top-level navigation is limited.

Creating navigation this simple and elegant is a very difficult job. There are people who specialize in helping companies do that. They are called library scientists or information architects. Information architects specialize in understanding both information and how humans process it. They need to understand both your audience and the terms that are common in your industry.

That is crucial to your navigation. You need to use terms and phrases that your customers understand intuitively. It doesn't matter what the term means outside the context of your Web site as long as it is clear in the context of your site. For example, you would be very surprised if a "beds and bedding" link on my sample dog-toys Web site took you to a page talking about garden beds and how to grow bedding plants. You would expect the page to be about dog beds.

There's one part of navigation that most people forget: error pages. Error pages are the navigation that isn't seen by employees and Web designers in a company. Why? Because you know where your pages are and know how to get to them. You're not very likely to type in a URL on your own site, because you know that in three clicks you can be at the page. And even when you do type in a URL, if you mistype it, you're focused on where you're trying to go and so the error page is completely ignored.

But don't forget error pages when planning and building your navigation. Plan for three types of error pages:

TOOLS YOU NEED

▶ A good place to start with navigation on a Web page is by looking at the organization of your company. My article "Let Your Organization Reflect Your Site Layout" (http://about.com/webdesign/organization) talks about some common navigation elements that you can use as a starting place for your site. Once you've had it running for a while, talk to your customers. If they find the navigation easy to use, then there's no need to change it. Otherwise, you should start tweaking.

- **404 Page Not Found:** These show up when a link is bad or the URL is mistyped.
- **500 Internal Server Error:** This happens when your server is running a program and it breaks.
- **401 Unauthorized Page:** These pages tell your customers they have given an invalid username or password on a password-protect page.

Navigation Schemes

Every site needs access points, signposts, and maps, but the amount you have of each depends upon the size and structure of your Web site.

A site like mine, with thousands of pages, needs a lot more access points and maps than a site with only twenty pages. But it's all relative. When I first started on About.com, my site had only a couple hundred pages. At that time most of my access points were in the left column, but rather than having eighteen to twenty separate categories, I had around ten. As my site has grown in size and complexity, I've added more items to my access points, and my maps have grown more and more complex.

Top-level navigation is the most important navigation on your site. Top-level navigation elements should be on every page of your site. Most people prefer navigation that remains consistent in naming and the location on the page.

Top-level navigation includes the main site sections on a Web site. In general, it's a good idea to limit it to no more than seven to ten links. You want there to be enough information in the sections that your customers can find what they're looking for without spending a lot of time looking.

Narrowing your top-level navigation down to a small number of links can be very challenging. It's something that About.com has

TOOLS YOU NEED

▶ If you want a quick overview of all the different status codes that your server can send to a Web browser, check out my "HTTP Status Codes" page (http://about .com/webdesign/httpstatus codes). Most of the time, a Web page will return a status code of "200 OK," and you see the Web page. But if it doesn't return that status, you can find out more about what the different codes mean.

been struggling with for years. I have eighteen top-level categories, where most of my articles and information are stored, and that's a lot.

Second-level navigation can be handled in many ways. One of the more popular methods is to create a dynamic menu that appears as you mouse over the top-level navigation. It is possible to do this with standards-based design. As long as you're careful, this type of navigation can work well on a Web site. This style of second-level navigation works well when you have a lot of categories that are very clearly related to one another.

Another option for second-level navigation is to leave it visible on the page at all times, as About.com does. This can result in a cluttered page, but if your site has a huge amount of information this can be the only way to make it visible. You see this style most commonly on sites where there are a huge number of categories or with topics that have several jargon terms that all mean the same thing. For example, on a computer site someone looking for monitors might search for "CRT," "monitor," or "flat screen"—and any of those terms could be used in the navigation.

Many large corporate sites have second-level navigation that changes depending upon where you are on their site. This works well if you have site segments that are very separate from each other. For example, a corporation might have a site section for enterprise customers and another section for consumers. Consumers aren't going to care about site licensing, but that might be the most important part of an enterprise-focused site.

Breadcrumbs tell people where they are. The challenge with Web pages is that, unlike a physical location, it's hard to tell where you are in the greater site context. This becomes truer as the Web

ELSEWHERE ON THE WEB

▶ If you're interested in seeing what my site or many other sites looked like years ago, you can use the Internet Archive Wayback Machine (www.archive.org/web/web .php). Here are two caveats if you want to check out my site, however. First, it was originally just the HTML site; Jean Kaiser ran the Web Design site. Second, the archive only has pictures dating back to 1999 for my site, and by that time I had a few more than ten category links.

▶ Every page on your site has the potential of being an ambassador for your Web site; think of every page as a potential entry page. If your signposts and top-level navigation don't tell your customers where they are and how to get to other places on your site, you'll lose them. In my article "Every Page Is an Entry Page" (http://about .com/webdesign/entrypage), I talk about how to make sure that all your Web pages help your customer to stay and be comfortable on your Web site, rather than inviting them in and then sending them away.

gets more and more diverse. In many cases, the home page is no longer the only place that someone might enter a Web site.

If someone does a search and ends up on an article or product page on your site, will they know where they are? That kind of identification includes more than your company logo. Will they be able to find related products, services, or articles? Will it be clear that this article or product is part of a bigger category or site?

Web site signposts provide information to your readers so that they know where they are. At the most basic level, a signpost can be your company logo and a page title. But a good signpost system will include more than the "You are here" found on most mall maps. You'll also want to tell people where they are in the site structure and how that relates to other articles and information on your site. That is what breadcrumb trails are for.

Every page of my About.com Web Design/HTML site has a breadcrumb trail. At the very top of a typical article page are the words "You are here." This is followed by the breadcrumb that orients you on both my Web Design site and within the entire About.com hierarchy. For example, on my article "CSS Outline Styles" (http://about.com/webdesign/cssoutlines), the breadcrumb trail reads: "You are here: About > Computing & Technology > Web Design / HTML > CSS > Advanced CSS > CSS Outlines— They Are More Than Just Another Border." This tells you that this article is in the Advanced CSS category, which is a sub-category of the CSS category, which is part of my Web Design/HTML site, which is in the Computing & Technology channel on About.com.

If you click the breadcrumb to enter the Advanced CSS category (http://about.com/webdesign/advancedcss), you see an example where About.com uses a second breadcrumb trail. In this case, the second breadcrumb appears below the About.com logo and site title in the content area of the page. For the Advanced CSS page it reads "> CSS > Advanced CSS > Advanced Cascading

Style Sheets (CSS)." This was added to categories and subcategories to provide some additional navigation within our map pages. Our categories can get very complicated. We can have up to nine subcategories on any top-level category, so having a second form of breadcrumb makes the pages easier to follow.

Building a breadcrumb trail for every page on your site can be a huge chore especially if your site is not in a database or **content management** system (CMS). Many blogging tools will build breadcrumbs from your categories and place them on the pages automatically. I've found that building a site by hand with a breadcrumb trail quickly becomes tedious. If you don't have a database or CMS to help you maintain your categories and breadcrumb trail, I recommend keeping your trail simple and only linking to the top-level navigation pages that relate to each sub-page. Once you start needing multiple levels in your breadcrumb, you'll also have a site that's big enough to need a database.

An easier way to build in signpost navigation is by using "You are here" type markers in your top-level navigation. This is done by changing the color of the navigation element when you are on pages that fall in that category. Later on in this chapter, I'll show you how to do that using CSS and standards-based design.

Maps are the Swiss army knife of your Web-site navigation. They can be as big or as small as you need them to be. I have some map pages that only have two or three links on them and one "Site Map" page that links to every page in my site.

The key to map pages is to make sure they provide the information that your customer is looking for on that particular subject. For example, you might have a navigation page that lists all your products or all your articles on a specific topic. About.com calls these "Category" pages; we can link to both our own articles and articles from outside our site.

ASK YOUR GUIDE

Why is it called a breadcrumb or breadcrumb trail?

▶ On most Web sites, the point of a breadcrumb trail is to show the reader the way back to the home page. Like Hansel and Gretel's fairy tale breadcrumb trail, the links in the trail show the way back. Though the term implies that the site knows how you arrived, most breadcrumb trails are static and reference the most common path to the page you are on.

Error Pages

Many Web designers forget to edit their error-message pages. Because of that, they are missing out on a huge opportunity to help their customers navigate better through their Web site.

404 Error or Page Not Found is the most common error. Compare the following two error pages. Which do you find more useful?

ELSEWHERE ON THE WEB

▶ A lot of Web designers out there have too much time on their hands. Not only do they write great-looking sites, they also develop amusing, interesting, and useful 404 pages. The 404 Research Lab (www.404lab.com/404) collects 404 error message pages for us to read and enjoy. Haiku on 404 pages is only the beginning.

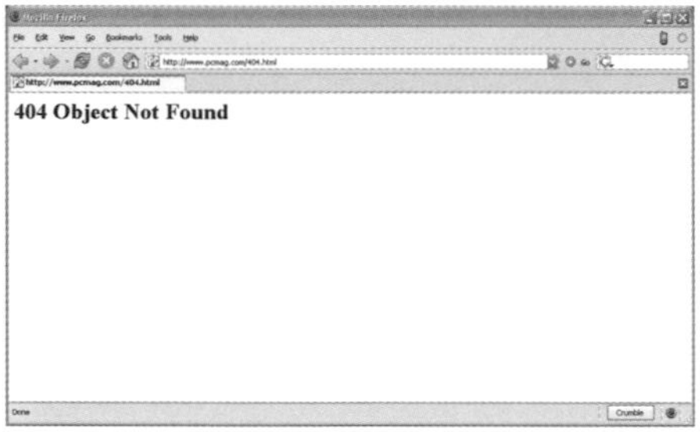

Figure 8-1: Page not found at PC Magazine (www.pcmag.com)

Figure 8-2: Page not found at the Motley Fool (www.fool.com)

The page on **www.pcmag.com** shows a very simple 404 Error message page. Customers who mistype a URL on the Motley Fool Web site are given a lot more information and help.

While your boss, CEO, coworkers, and employees don't see the 404 page very often, your customers will see it a lot. Make sure it has useful information. Here are a few tips for writing a good 404 error page:

- **Keep the tone of your error page similar to the rest of your site.** If content (such as jokes) is out of place on your normal site pages, it doesn't belong on a 404 error page, either.
- **Give your customers options to find what they are looking for.** But don't forget that they probably don't know exactly what they were looking for. If they clicked on a link from another site, they won't know what they were going to get. Remember that bad links will make most people leave no matter how engaging your 404 page is.
- **Place a search box on the page** so that your customers can search for what they were looking for.
- **Include links to your major site sections.** If you have a small site, include your entire site map on the 404 page, but don't forget to maintain it as your site grows.
- **Don't expect your customers to report the error.** Yes, there are a few good people out there who will, but most won't have the time or inclination. Plus, if you have access to your error logs, you should be able to tell both where they were coming from (the **referrer**) and what page they didn't find.
- **If you want users to report the error, make that as easy as possible.** Include a form on the 404 page. Fill in the referrer and the bad URL for them so that they don't have to. And be sure to act on these reports. I have a couple of readers who volunteer their time checking links on my site, all because I responded with thanks the first time they did so.

TOOLS YOU NEED

▶ Customizing your 404 page depends a lot upon what Web server you have. If you are on an Apache Web server, follow the instructions in my article "How to Create a Custom 404 Page on Apache" (http://about .com/webdesign/404apache). And for more tips on making your 404 page useful, check out my article "How Useful Is Your 404 Page?" (http:// about.com/webdesign/use ful404).

You also might need a 500 error page and a 401 unauthorized error page. The 500 error appears when a program on your Web server fails in some way. If you use CGI or other server-side scripts on your Web site, there is a possibility that one of them will have a problem executing. The 500 server error page should give suggestions for what your customers can do if a program breaks.

The 401 unauthorized error page is used when you have password protection on your Web site. If your customers fill in an invalid username or password too many times, the server will respond with the 401 unauthorized message. You can use this page to give suggestions on how to get a new password sent or what to do to get reauthorized.

Coding Standards-Based Navigation

As designers get more and more comfortable building Web pages with CSS, many methods of doing things become more natural. Web navigation has traditionally been a series of paragraphs or table cells that make up the HTML for top-level navigation. But what is a standard navigation segment? It's a list. So for standards-based navigation we should use a list element, specifically an unordered list.

My sample Web site will have the following items in the navigation:

- **Home:** Takes you back to the home page
- **Dog Toys for Sale:** Links to my product pages
- **Dog Information:** Leads to articles
- **About This Site:** Contains all the site information pages (as described in Chapter 7)

The HTML I'll use looks like this:

```
<ul id="navigation">
```

```
<li><a href="/index.html">Home</a></li>
<li><a href="/products/index.html">Dog Toys for
Sale</a></li>
<li><a href="/articles/index.html">Dog Informa-
tion</a></li>
<li><a href="/about/index.html">About This
Site</a></li>
</ul>
```

Using that HTML, I can create a navigation system that is as fancy as I need it to be.

First let's create a vertical navigation system. If you viewed the above HTML without any styles, it looks like a bulleted list, so the first thing we should do is get rid of the bullets. Notice that in the CSS I am only styling the unordered list that is identified as "navigation" (ul#navigation). If I used "ul" as my **selector**, then every list on the page would look like my navigation. I also want to get rid of the spacing that browsers tend to leave around lists so I'll clear out the margin and padding on the tag as well. In my CSS document (shown in Example 8-1, http://about.com/web design/example8-1code), I write:

```
ul#navigation {
  list-style: none;
  margin: 0;
  padding: 0;
}
```

The nice thing about vertical menus is that the UL elements stack vertically. Therefore, the next thing I'll do is make each list element look like a box. I'll put this CSS into my document (online Example 8-2, http://about.com/webdesign/example8-2code):

```
ul#navigation li { margin: .1em 0; }
```

TOOLS YOU NEED

▶ If you're using an Apache Web server to run your Web site, it is easy to set up password-protected directories. The trick is that password protection is done with a separate program; you need to use htaccess. My how-to file on htaccess (http://about.com/web design/htaccess) walks you through the steps to get it up and running on your site. In less than fifteen minutes, you can have a password-protected area of your Apache Web site.

```
ul#navigation li a {
  display: block;
  width: 175px;
  height: 20px;
  border: .1em solid #3c6;
  text-decoration: none;
  color: #63c;
  font-weight: bold;
  text-align: center;
}
```

ELSEWHERE ON THE WEB

▶ If you don't know how to create a gradient in your graphics software, the About.com Graphics Software Guide explains how to use Photoshop to create a gradient (http://about.com/graphicssoft/photoshopgradient). She also has a tutorial for creating interesting gradients with PhotoImpact (http://about.com/graphicssoft/photoimpactgradient).

`display: block;` tells the browser that the anchor inside our navigation list is a block-level element, rather than an inline element. This makes the entire box clickable and not just the text. When you're making navigation that looks like buttons, you want to make sure that the entire box is clickable. The width, height, and border properties set the width, height, and border of the list items. Then the text-decoration removes the underline from the anchor tag. Finally, the color, font-weight, and text-align adjust the type in the navigation to what we want.

But it doesn't look like navigation yet. In online Example 8-3 (**http://about.com/webdesign/example8-3code**), I added some color to the navigation boxes. When you mouse over the boxes, they change color. You can see the CSS for that online.

To make this navigation more interesting, I used a small image with a color gradient for the background color. As in Example 8-3, I used a second color gradient image in Example 8-4 when you put your mouse over the navigation button.

The CSS for Example 8-4 is online (**http://about.com/webdesign/example8-4code**). I added the gradient images with these lines:

```
ul#navigation li a { background: #fff
url(navbg.gif); }
ul#navigation li a:hover { background: #fff
url(navbg_over.gif); }
```

I then uploaded the two images (navbg.gif and navbg_over.gif) to the server in the same directory as the Web pages.

But what about a horizontal navigation menu? Vertical menus are fairly easy because a list is a vertical item. But horizontal menus are easy as well. You can take the exact same HTML as in the previous examples and create a horizontal menu with just a few changes to the CSS. To create the horizontal menu in online Example 8-5 (**http://about.com/webdesign/example8-5code**), all I did was add `float: left;` to the ul#navigation li property. I also changed the margins on that same property to have the spacing on the left and right of the buttons, not the top and bottom.

Adding signposts to CSS navigation is easy, too. It's a good idea to use your navigation to help your customers know where they are. The most common way to do that is to change the color of the current navigation item so that it's highlighted. To add signposts to the navigation on my sample site, we need to modify the HTML a little bit to tell the Web browser where (in which tab) the current page is located. For example, if your current page is in the articles section, you would change the HTML to this:

```
<ul id="navigation">
<li><a href="/index.html">Home</a></li>
<li><a href="/products/index.html">Dog Toys for
Sale</a></li>
<li id="youarehere"><a href="/articles/index.
html">Dog Information</a></li>
<li><a href="/about/index.html">About This
Site</a></li>
</ul>
```

Notice that there is now a `id="youarehere"` attribute in the "Dog Information" list item.

To set the highlight, change the background color for the selector ul#navigation li#youarehere a. I decided to remove the change of color from the hover state and instead make that the highlight color. But to make it clear that these are links, I added an underline when you mouse over it. You can see the results online at Example 8-6 (http://about.com/webdesign/example8-6code). Be sure to click on the different links to see how the highlight color follows where you are on the site (because on each page, I changed the location of the id="youarehere" attribute). The final CSS looks like this:

```
ul#navigation {
  list-style: none;
  margin: 0;
  padding: 0;
}
ul#navigation li { margin: 0 .1em; float: left; }
ul#navigation li a {
  display: block;
  width: 175px;
  height: 20px;
  text-decoration: none;
  color: #63c;
  font-weight: bold;
  text-align: center;
  background: #fff url(navbg.gif);
}
ul#navigation li a:hover { text-decoration:
underline; color: #000; }
ul#navigation li#youarehere a { background: #fff
url(navbg_over.gif); color: #000; }
```

Test Your Navigation with Customers

Once you have the navigation you want, test it with your customers. If a navigation element, style, or term doesn't work, don't hesitate to change it. Unlike print, you can make mistakes and fix them, and most of your readers will never know.

A/B testing is a good idea. With A/B testing, you can see how two or more design ideas work relative to one another. One design is your control—perhaps the navigation currently live on your site. The second design is what you'd like to test. You set up your Web site so that half of your customers see design A and the other half sees design B. There are many ways to do this, but the easiest is to hire a company to do it for you.

In order to make A/B testing effective, you need to determine what you are testing for. You need to come up with metrics to measure so that you can determine if design B is working better than design A. For example, in testing navigation, you might track how many people in each design used search versus how many clicked through your navigation. If you believe that your new navigation should be more effective and more available than search, then the new design should have more clicks to the navigation versus search than the old design has.

The advantage of A/B testing is that it gives you the chance to test new designs without disrupting your site completely. Also, if it turns out that the new design doesn't work as well as the old design, you can always turn it off.

If you can't do A/B testing, do some testing. Another way to test new navigation is to add it to some of the pages of your site, but not all. This doesn't give you as good a sense of how it will perform overall, but it is easier to implement.

Survey your customers to find out what customers think of the new navigation. Surveys are a great way to get the pulse of your readers, and with free CGI scripts, they can be an inexpensive way to determine if your new navigation is working.

ELSEWHERE ON THE WEB

▶ Once you have a standard top-level navigation with signposts in place, it's not hard to move to extended menus. These are menus where the second (and third and fourth, etc.) levels slide out when you put your mouse over them. A great site to get ideas and help with menus is the "CSS Showcase" (www.alvit.de/css-showcase/css-navigation-techniques-showcase.php). Most of the extended menus require some use of Java-Script to get them to work in IE 6, but they do create a nice effect.

Get Linked

Navigation is a very important part of a Web site. These links from my site go over more of what you need to know about building and maintaining Web navigation.

WRITING WEB NAVIGATION

Web navigation is fun! There are so many ways to do it. And just because you've chosen one way doesn't mean you can't choose others, too. These links cover how to build and maintain a Web navigation system that works for your site.

↗ http://about.com/webdesign/navigationindex

HTTP

The HyperText Transport Protocol, or HTTP, is what makes the Web work and what differentiates it from e-mail or FTP. These links will help you better understand HTTP including the status and error codes.

↗ http://about.com/webdesign/httpindex

FREE MENU TEMPLATES

These free menu templates show you how to build CSS, standards-based Web-navigation menus.

↗ http://about.com/webdesign/menutemplates

Chapter 9

Building Your Home Page

There's No Second Chance to Make a First Impression

This adage is as true in home pages as it is in life. Your home page is what sells your company to your customer. It is what your potential partners and investors see when they evaluate your company. It is what all of your marketing and PR brochures advertise.

Your customers don't care about you or your products.

That may seem harsh, but it's true. People surf the Web for many different reasons: for entertainment, to find reference and comparison information, and to do their shopping. Unless they are participating in a focus group (or work for the company in question), most people don't think much about the Web pages they are on beyond asking this question: Does this Web site meet my needs of this moment? Their momentary needs might be any of the following:

- To find a link to kitchen timers for sale
- To find reviews of kitchen timers
- To read other opinions of the kitchen timer they bought
- To find the return policy to return the kitchen timer
- To read instructions on how to use the kitchen timer
- To suggest new uses for their kitchen timer
- To participate in a game using a kitchen timer

Some of these examples are silly, but if your site sells kitchen timers, you should have the most useful options right on your home page. At the very least, make it clear that your site caters to kitchen-timer lovers.

What should you have on your home page? This can be a challenge, especially for a company that sells a lot of products or has a lot of articles on different topics. All home pages should accomplish at least a few basic things:

- **Summarize the purpose of the site.** Many companies leave this off of their home page because they have so many other things they want to say or sell. But don't assume that everyone landing on your home page will automatically know what your company does. Your summary doesn't have to be long, and it doesn't even have to be text. Google summarizes its site with a search box.
- **Put up links to the products, services, or articles that are available on your Web site.** If you have a lot of articles or products, then you will have more links on your home page. You want to communicate the scope of your site from your home page. Also, make sure that you link to your most popular products or articles somewhere on the page. If you are

running a site called **www.kitchentimersforsale.com**, and you don't have a link to kitchen timers for sale, you will confuse your customers.

- **Link information pages from your home page.** These are the contact pages, legal pages, and so on (as discussed in Chapter 7). But don't fall into the PR department morass. This is where departments like PR, legal, or investor relations want you to have multiple links to their content on the home page. Yes, link to those areas of your site, but don't turn your home page into a press center. Most of the visitors to your Web site are not members of the press, investors, or interested in your copyright and other legal notices. Put up one or two links to those areas of your site and no more.

The Page Many People Never See

It's interesting to me that when someone sets out to build a Web site, what she thinks of is the home page. In my design gallery (**http://about.com/webdesign/designgallery**), I'm always sent to the home page rather than an interior page. The home page usually has the most effort put into it by the design firm, gets the most page views as well as the most attention from the marketing department, and is the only page your CEO would ever call you about if it were broken. The home page is the most important page on your Web site.

But is it the most important? Before we start thinking about the home page, let's examine this premise. The home page is the page that represents your company. It provides information to your customers about your products, services, articles, press releases, and stock prices. In many ways, the home page attempts to represent a tiny slice of each portion of your Web site. Your home page has to be all things to all people, or at least most things to most people.

Some of your customers never look at your home page. While it may get the most page views of any single page, that doesn't mean that everyone sees it. I have seen this on two different Web sites I've managed. On the first, we tracked average page views per visit. We found that most visitors came to the site, read an article, and left—one page view per visit. While the home page got a lot of page views, other pages on the site got a lot as well. On the second site, we tracked the path customers took from the home page as well as the length of time they spent on the home page. In this case, something like 70 percent of the people arrived on the home page, looked for a specific link, and clicked on it when they found it. They were not on the home page any longer than it took to skim the page for a link and click away.

On the first site, the customers never saw the home page at all. They arrived at the site by way of search engines to find the answer to a specific question. Once they had read the page, they left without scanning the rest of the site. On the second site, customers were coming to the home page, but the analytics evidence (and focus groups) showed that they were only on the page long enough to find the link they wanted before they clicked away. They may have landed on the home page, but they never saw any of it.

Your home page serves many purposes and many masters. Though it is difficult to pin down a single goal of the home page, some of the more common goals include the following:

- Detail the products or services available
- Promote different areas of the company
- Provide investor information

- Include interesting content
- Highlight sales and promotions
- Offer ways to find more content on the site
- Provide navigation to other languages or regional site versions
- Show how cool or innovative the company is

Home pages do a lot because they have a lot to do.

Be Selective in What Goes on the Home Page

Selectivity is the key to a good home page. This applies to content and design elements. Do not focus on technology unless you are in the business of selling that technology.

Just because your company has the department, doesn't mean it should be on the home page. This is a common problem with corporations. Every department team wants a link and a short description on the home page so that people will come to their pages and buy their products. I have seen this at companies that sell only two things and at companies where there are 700-plus categories to choose from. (About.com has this issue.)

You need to think about what your customers are looking for. There is always a need to help your customers find something in addition to what they are looking for, but that is secondary. Your home page has two goals: to provide a brief introduction of your company to your customers and to provide navigation so that your customers can find what they want. The first goal isn't as important as the second.

Google did it best when they built their home page. As a Google customer, I know exactly what to do—I go there, enter my search terms, and find what I am looking for. There are a few other links on the page, but the primary focus is the logo and the search box below it. Google designers recognized that their customers don't care about their other offerings as much as they care about searching. So Google pulled it out and left everything else for sub-pages on the site.

However, Google is the exception, not the rule. Most Web designs seem to deliberately hide what the customer most wants from the site. For example, if you look at the McAfee security Web site (www.mcafee.com/us), what is the focus of the page?

Obviously, the designers want us to focus more on the graphics and short description of the company than on what you can do on the site or where you can go. Customers have to self-segment into "Home & Home Office" users, "Small Business" customers, and so on. The segments open up when you mouse over them to display links specific to that customer type. But customers still have to read the segment headers, decide which applies to them, and then click on the appropriate link. Compared to Google, that is a lot of work.

Now, I don't know what McAfee customers are looking for when they come to the site, but as I was writing this chapter, I did have anti-virus software that needed to be renewed. So I went to the McAfee site to see how much their anti-virus software costs and to compare it to the software I currently have. Unfortunately, in my quick scan of the page, I didn't see any sign of the term "anti-virus," so I went back to Google and typed that into the search box. For the typical McAfee customer, that would have been a fairly frustrating trip to the company's home page.

If you're doing a redesign, look at your Web-site logs. In many ways redesigning a home page is a lot easier than building one from scratch. You can look at what is and isn't working on your current home page and keep the good stuff while removing the bad.

On my site, I use my Web logs in two ways. The first is to see what text people click on. I will change the text of links to see if that causes an upswing or a downswing on the clicks to that page. For example, in the home-page navigation on my About.com Web Design/HTML site, I determined that people were more likely to click on "HTML Tutorials" than on "Beginning HTML," so now I use "HTML/Web Design Tutorials" (though I'm thinking of testing another phrase in its place). The other way to use your statistics is to look at what pages are most popular on your Web site. If these pages also correlate to a specific search term you see in the statistics, then use that term to link to the page. Why fight it? If your customers want that information, trying to hide it is only going to annoy them or drive them away from your Web site.

Keep only what's essential. Only three things are essential to a home page:

- Explaining what your company is about
- Helping your customers find what they are looking for
- Showing off the content available

Explaining what your company is about shouldn't be more than a sentence or two and a branding logo. You need to be able to boil down what your company offers into fifteen words or less. Include that language on the visible part of your home page, but also make sure that your title tag includes the same information. A good title tag has the title at the front and then a short description of the site following it.

```
<title>Dogs and Their Toys—Buy Dog Toys Online
and Get Information About Dogs—Dogs and Their
Toys</title>
```

Make sure that you include a search box on your home page. This way, visitors can perform a search to find the specific element of your site they need. Highlight those things that are most popular or heavily used on your site so that your customers can go right to them.

Finally, you need to make sure that your readers know what is available on your Web site. The best way to do this is to have small snippets of content on the home page. But if you don't have the real estate available, or you have a lot of content, make sure you have links so that they can navigate around your site.

Be careful about the images you use on your home page. Many people automatically assume that all graphics are ads and don't even look at them. If you have content or navigation hidden in images, your customers may not be seeing it. Make sure your home-page images serve a purpose.

You Have Seven to Ten Seconds

Your home page is the most visited page on your Web site, but unless you are as minimalist as Google, it won't always have what your customers are looking for. You have to hook them into your Web page and make them want to look through it to find what they are looking for. If you don't hook them within ten seconds of going to your Web site, they've hit the "Back" button and are looking elsewhere.

More than any other Web page on your site, your home page must load as quickly as possible. The seven to ten seconds you have to hook your customers starts the instant that they click on a link to your site. If it takes six seconds for your home page to load usable content, you've got only a few seconds left.

ELSEWHERE ON THE WEB

▶ If you're interested in creating a good home page, take some hints from bad ones. Vincent Flanders' site "Web Pages That Suck" (www.webpagesthatsuck.com) covers all you could ever want to know about how to create a bad, ugly, unusable Web page.

Chapter 12 explains more about how to help your site download faster, but here are some tips:

- Keep your images and multimedia as small as possible. I like to limit images to no more than 5 to 10KB, with a maximum of 30KB total per page.
- Avoid using ads from external Web sites on your home page. You can't control how fast another server will serve content, and you don't want ads to slow down your page.
- Write your HTML in sections so that even as the lower portion of the page is loading the top is done and readable.

Types of Home-Page Layouts

There are only three types of home-page layouts on the Web. Unless you're doing something incredibly new and groundbreaking, chances are your Web site will have one of them:

- Splash pages are pages where the customer is treated to some type of visual media before being directed (either automatically or by click) to the main content of the Web site.
- Information-centered home pages focus on immediately getting content to the customers.
- Navigation-centered home pages focus on displaying the breadth of the Web site through links and other navigation.

I do not like splash pages. Splash pages are put up for one purpose: to show off. Except in rare instances, splash pages don't provide any information about the Web site; instead, they are just a fancy advertisement for the site. If I want to watch an ad, I'll turn on the television, not click on a link.

But there are some good, less emotional reasons to avoid them:

TOOLS YOU NEED

▶ If you're looking for more tips on how to speed up your home page, I have a number of them in my article "Tips for Speeding Up Your Web Page" (http://about.com/web design/quicktipsspeed). There are so many elements to Web pages that it can take a lot of effort to improve your download speed. But if you focus on these tips and read Chapter 12, you can make sure your home page is a fast loader.

▶ If you're still determined to build a splash page, I discuss them in more detail in my article "Splash Pages—Pros and Cons" (http://about.com/webdesign/splashpages). There you can find out some of the potential benefits to splash pages as well as tips for building them.

- The usability of a splash-page home page is completely flawed. Visitors make a decision to come to your home page. An advertisement about the page does nothing but annoy them and make them click again (at best) or annoy them and drive them away (at worst).
- If you must have a splash page, be sure to test it with your customers. In some studies, between 16 and 71 percent of customers bail out after seeing a splash page and don't visit any other pages on the site.
- Search engines don't like splash pages. While it is possible to design splash pages that search engines can read, the reality is that you're not going to get the same level of **SEO** with a splash page as with a content-rich home page.
- Splash pages can seem pretentious. Instead of providing information to your readers in a way that works for them, they are built to show off and salve the egos of the designers.
- Splash pages make the whole site seem slower. Note that one splash page isn't going to affect the actual download times of the rest of your Web site. But a splash page can take longer to run than downloading and viewing a standard Web page. This is because while the page itself may load quickly, your customers then have to wade through the entire animation process or search for the "skip" link. They aren't doing what they want to do right away, so the whole site seems slower to them.

Information-centered home pages are perfect for small sites. When you don't have a lot of content, either because you're starting out or because you only sell one thing, an information-centered home page is the perfect place to start. In this case, the information should be the primary focus of the page. There will be links on an information-centered page, but you'll meet the three guidelines (explaining what your company is about, helping your customers find what they want, and showcasing your content) by providing more content on the home page instead.

For my dog-toys home page, I'm going to use a large logo at the top, with my site headline and a short paragraph at the top that explains the company. The HTML is fairly simple; the head of the document is longer than the headline and promo text.

```
<!DOCTYPE html PUBLIC "-//W3C//DTD XHTML 1.0
Transitional//EN"
  "http://www.w3.org/TR/xhtml1/DTD/xhtml1-tran-
sitional.dtd">
<html>
<head>
<title>Dogs and Their Toys - Buy Dog Toys and
Get Dog Info at Dogs and Their Toys</title>
<meta name="keywords" content="dog toys, dog
information, help with dogs, dog collars, dog
equipment" />
<meta name="description" content="Find the best
dog toys and dog information at Dogs and Their
Toys" />
<link type="text/css" href="zexample9-1.css"
rel="stylesheet" />
</head>
<body>
<div id="container">
<h1>Dogs and Their Toys</h1>
<h2>Find the best dog toys and dog information
at Dogs and Their Toys.</h2>
</div>
</body>
</html>
```

The CSS defines how it will look. You can see this first portion of the home page, as well as the CSS, online in Example 9-1 (http://about.com/webdesign/example9-1code).

Next I want to add navigation and some space for my content. I want the rest of the page to have two columns. The HTML looks a lot like that on page 145:

```
<!DOCTYPE html PUBLIC "-//W3C//DTD XHTML 1.0
Transitional//EN"
  "http://www.w3.org/TR/xhtml1/DTD/xhtml1-tran-
sitional.dtd">
<html>
<head>
<title>Dogs and Their Toys - Buy Dog Toys and
Get Dog Info at Dogs and Their Toys</title>
<meta name="keywords" content="dog toys, dog
information, help with dogs, dog collars, dog
equipment" />
<meta name="description" content="Find the best
dog toys and dog information at Dogs and Their
Toys" />
<link type="text/css" href="zexample9-2.css"
rel="stylesheet" />
</head>
<body>
<div id="container">
<div id="header">
<h1>Dogs and Their Toys</h1>
<h2>Find the best dog toys and dog information
at Dogs and Their Toys.</h2>
</div>
<ul id="navigation">
<li><a href="/" class="here">Home</a></li>
<li><a href="/products/">Dog Toys for Sale</a></
li>
<li><a href="/articles/">Dog Information</a></
li>
<li><a href="/about/">About This Site</a></li>
</ul>
<div id="main">
<div id="primary">
<h3>Headline 2</h3>
<p>Text goes here</p>
</div>
```

```
<div id="secondary">
<h3>Headline 3</h3>
<ul>
<li>bulleted list</li>
<li>bulleted list</li>
<li>bulleted list</li>
</ul>
</div></div></div>
</body>
</html>
```

With the CSS, the page ends up looking like this:

Figure 9-1: The home page is coming along

You can see the HTML and CSS codes online in Example 9-2 (http://about.com/webdesign/example9-2code).

I then created the page shown in online Example 9-3 (http://about.com/webdesign/example9-3code) with some actual content so that you could see how the Web page looks with real text and images. As you can see, there's a product promotion as well as an article with a link to the article index and product pages.

Figure 9-2: The home page with content

Use a navigation home page when you have a lot of content to promote. One of the key features of a home page is to display the content for your readers to find. For our navigation-focused home page, I'm going to create a three-column layout with a header and footer. That will give you a lot more space to put navigation links, content links, and some content on your home page. The HTML is based on the three-column header and footer layout from my free Web templates (**http://about.com/webdesign/3colheadfoot**).

```
<!DOCTYPE html PUBLIC "-//W3C//DTD XHTML 1.0
Transitional//EN"
"http://www.w3.org/TR/xhtml1/DTD/xhtml1-transi-
tional.dtd">
<html>
<head>
<title>Dogs and Their Toys - Buy Dog Toys and
Get Dog Info at Dogs and Their Toys</title>
<meta name="keywords" content="dog toys, dog
information, help with dogs, dog collars, dog
equipment" />
<meta name="description" content="Find the best dog
toys and dog information at Dogs and Their Toys" />
<link type="text/css" href="zexample9-4.css"
rel="stylesheet" />
```

```
</head>
<body>
<div id="header">
<h1>Dogs and Their Toys</h1>
<ul id="navigation">
<li><a href="/" class="here">Home</a></li>
<li><a href="/products/">Dog Toys for Sale</a></li>
<li><a href="/articles/">Dog Information</a></li>
<li><a href="/about/">About This Site</a></li>
</ul>
</div>
<div id="container">
<div id="main-holder">
<div id="main">
<p>main column</p>
</div>
<div id="subnav">
<p>left column</p>
</div>
</div>
<div id="extra">
<p>right column</p>
</div>
</div>
<div id="footer">
<p>footer</p>
</div>
</body>
</html>
```

Figure 9-3: Take a look at
the navigation

If you look at the page, you'll notice that the navigation is the reverse of what you might expect. This is because I used a `float: right;` on the navigation list to get it to line up on the right side of the page. See the full CSS online in Example 9-4 (**http://about .com/webdesign/example9-4code**).

The browser looks at all the elements in the list and floats them one after the other in order from right to left. Now, an easy way to fix that would be to change the order of the navigation list so that "Home" comes last and "About This Site" comes first. But if in your next redesign you decide to position the navigation to the left side, you have to go in and change the HTML.

To fix this, I decided to forgo the precise placement of my navigation bar and instead position it using padding. The drawback to this method is that on smaller windows there is now a horizontal scroll bar, though if you scroll to the right nothing appears to be there. While this isn't ideal, it isn't a major issue for now. If the site eventually needs a fourth column (such as for ads), that extended line and scroll bar won't look out of place at all. The CSS I changed looks like this:

```
#header #navigation {
 float: left;
 background: transparent url(paws.gif) no-repeat 150px;
 color: #fff;
 width: 800px;
 font-size: 0.75em;
 /* for IE 6 and 5 */
 margin: 48px 0 0 180px;
}
/* IE 6 and 5 can't read this property */
#header > #navigation {
 padding: 0 0 0 350px;
 margin: 48px 0 0 0px;
}
#header ul#navigation li a {
 padding: .25em 1em;
 margin: 0 1em 0 .25em;
```

```
    background-color: #183;
    color: #fff;
    text-decoration: none;
    float: left;
}
```

Get the full HTML and CSS online in Example 9-5 (http://about.
com/webdesign/example9-5code).

Figure 9-4: The final
version of the home page

ELSEWHERE ON THE WEB

▶ Designing your site in CSS
makes it easy to keep doing
redesigns on your entire site.
Jared Spool of User Interface
Engineering wrote an interesting article about CSS and
iterative design (www.uie
.com/events/uiconf/articles/
iterative_design_css) that
explains how you can use
CSS to make small changes
to your site.

This layout focuses more on the links and available content,
but it also provides you with a large central section to promote
products or announce new articles.

**Here's one last thing about designing your home
page.** Never stop modifying it. Once your home page is up,
start watching your log files. Update the link text or the colors
or modify the location of elements on your page. The beauty of
Web design is that you never have to settle for something that
isn't working. Everything can be changed. Now that you've built
an entire site, you may be wondering, "Why are there still six
more chapters in this book?" The rest of the book will take you
through how to improve your home page and the rest of your
site.

Get Linked

Creating a home page is the most important part of building your Web site. Don't take it lightly. The following links from my About.com Web Design/HTML site will help you build the best home page you can.

BASICS OF WEB DESIGN

First, start by learning the basics of Web design.
http://about.com/webdesign/webdesignbasics

BEGINNING CSS

Once you know Web design, learn CSS. While most HTML editors will do a great job with the HTML, CSS is still better when you do it by hand.
http://about.com/webdesign/beginningcss

WRITE A WEB PAGE THAT MEETS YOUR CUSTOMERS' GOALS

If your home page meets your customers' goals, they will buy your products, read your articles, and tell their friends about you. If it doesn't, they won't stay long enough to even remember your company name.
http://about.com/webdesign/customer

Chapter 10

Search-Engine Optimization (SEO) and Site Promotion

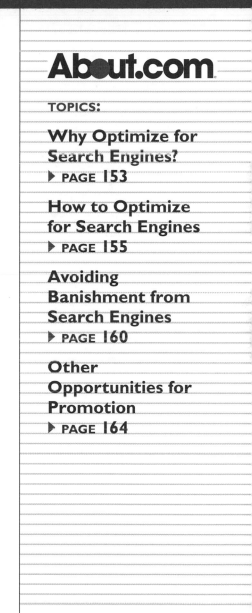

Why Optimize for Search Engines?

Many people are under the impression that optimizing a Web site for search engines is a way of tricking the search engines into rank-ing you higher. They equate the tool of SEO as being along the same lines as bribing a police officer or paying for votes. But the point of SEO is not to get something you don't deserve, but rather to write pages that have the optimal mix of keywords, content, and meta data. When someone wants to learn how to build a new doghouse, SEO is your way to get them to your Web page on building a doghouse rather than a page on something else.

Search engines only seem smart. In reality, search engines are only as smart as the people programming them. When people think about computers, they think "logical" and "methodical." This is true, but computers are also very literal. Search systems used to be so literal that if you typed in "computer," the search would only match on that word. Pages that had "computers" would not match the search.

When I was working at NETCOM, our search engine was of the very literal sort. If you put a phrase into the search engine, such as "netscape browser crashes," it would return with a list of every article on the site that had any of those three words in them. In the first iteration of the engine, it wouldn't even rank the results—if an article about goldfish was listed first in the search index and it mentioned crashes or Netscape, that would be the first result you'd see on the page. We did a lot to fix the search engine, but we weren't the programmers; all we could do was play with the ranking in the index and change things like using "AND" rather than "OR" when multiple terms were entered.

Search engines have come a long way since 1995, but they are still computers. And computers are not yet smarter than most humans. So, even though Google has a lot of sophisticated algorithms, it still can be hard to find information on a specific subject if you don't know the right words to use in your search.

A while ago, I was working on an article about URL parameters. These are the tags that come at the end of some URLs; they start with a question mark (?) and are separated by ampersands (&). For some reason, I couldn't think of the term "parameter." I ended up searching for thirty minutes or more using terms like "question mark in URL" and so on. I see this with my readers a lot, too—many people want to know how to include HTML from one document into another HTML document. But they search my site using terms like "use one page many times" and "write HTML once." If you don't know the term "include," it's hard to get meaningful search results that solve your problem.

ELSEWHERE ON THE WEB

▶ Luckily for us the founders of Google, one of the most popular search engines around, are very smart indeed. According to a profile on BBC (http://news.bbc .co.uk/1/hi/business/3666241 .stm), they were both doing doctorates in computer science at Stanford University when they dropped out of college to found Google.

SEO attempts to solve that problem. Yes, the goal of SEO is to get your pages ranked higher in the search engines. But you're not going to be highly ranked for every search term that anyone might type in. My husband Mark's site might be number-one in Google when you search for "computer reviews," but if you searched for "dressage saddles," his site wouldn't come up at all.

And that's appropriate. Mark writes the About.com PC Hardware/Reviews site (**http://compreviews.about.com/index.htm**). He doesn't have any information about horses or dressage or saddles, and he wouldn't want someone to come to his site looking for that. On the other hand, his site does have a huge number of computer reviews and information on PC hardware, so being optimized for the search term "computer reviews" is ideal for his site.

How to Optimize for Search Engines

SEO can be as easy or as hard as you want to make it. I only spend about thirty minutes per article on SEO. Other About.com Guides focus a lot more on making their pages as search-engine friendly as they possibly can. One Guide reviews his search terms every week and modifies his pages daily, including categories, page titles, link titles, and so on. He would review the terms more often, but we only get weekly reports. His site is one of the most popular on the network, so I wish I were willing to emulate him.

The following sections cover the six basic steps to optimizing a site for search engines.

Optimize each page separately. The key to SEO is to remember that every page of your site is an entry page. No matter how much you want everyone to start at your home page and click through your categories to the product or article they want to read, that isn't what's happening when someone arrives via a search engine.

In a random week, the first ten most popular search terms used to get to my site generated 4 percent of the traffic. That may not sound like a lot, but considering that I have thousands of search requests, that adds up to a lot of traffic. In that same week, my home page accounted for 8 percent of the traffic to the site. That means that search requests were nearly as common a way to enter my site as my home page. The top thirty-six referrals to my Web site were from search engines. I know from reviewing my stats over several years that this isn't a fluke—most people arrive at my site from search engines, and most of those search-engine hits take them to article pages, not my home page.

Optimize for a specific target phrase. The key to SEO is to choose a target phrase (or phrases, two to three at most) that you want to optimize your page for. There is no way that you'll be able to optimize a Web page for every possible way that someone might search for the topic, so you want to find one or two that you can incorporate into your page, and then own those terms.

For example, I wrote a Web page on how to make your Web page reload periodically (**http://about.com/webdesign/metarefresh**). There were a lot of terms I could have chosen: "http refresh," "meta redirect," or "automatic redirect." I decided to focus on the term "meta refresh." Because I didn't dilute my page with other search terms, I was able to get that page to number one in Google on a search for "meta refresh."

Here are a few tips on SEO:

- **Phrases work better than single words.** If one word is used a lot in searches for the topic (like "refresh" in my example above), include that in your phrase. But single words are very limiting and are hard to optimize for.

- **Make sure your target phrase is important.** Most of my article pages come up as well optimized for terms like "About .com" and "Jennifer Kyrnin," but other than my biography page or the "About Us" page on the site, these are not useful terms to optimize for because they are not what the page is about.
- **Your target phrase must be accurate to the content on the page.** As we'll see later, doing things to make your page come up on popular keyword phrases that aren't related to the page can hurt your rankings. You may get page views, but you won't get customers.
- **Your target phrase should be popular.** You want to find a phrase that people are searching for. On my site, when I was targeting the phrase "Beginning HTML" for my Beginning HTML Tutorials category (http://about.com/webdesign/ beginninghtml), I didn't get many page views until I switched the title and the phrase I was targeting to "HTML tutorials." In this case, the title still has "Beginning HTML" so I won't lose that search phrase, but "HTML tutorials" gets a lot more searches.

Analyze your competition. Unless you've invented something completely new and that's what your Web page is about, chances are that you have competition. While your site as a whole might compete with a specific site, your page-by-page competition can change. For example, my About.com Web Design/HTML site has competition from sites like W3Schools and WebReference, but my article on meta refresh also competes with an article on www .submitcorner.com and an article on Dan's Web Tips (http://webtips .dan.info).

WHAT'S HOT

▶ Figuring out the popular search terms can be challenging. My article "Search Engine Optimization Made Simple" (http://about.com/webdesign/ seopt) covers both the steps we're going through here, as well as some tools you can use to find popular search terms.

Once you have a target phrase, use it in Yahoo or Google or another search engine and see what pages come up. Take a look at your competition and analyze their pages:

- Do the pages that match that search term resemble what your page will be about? If they don't, you might want to think about a different phrase that is more targeted.
- How and where do they use the target phrase? You can use the cached version in Google to see your phrase words highlighted. To see your Google cache: search for your site in Google and then click on the "Cached" link below your result. If there is no "Cached" link, then Google doesn't have a cached copy of your site.
- Look at their page title and meta data. Is the phrase mentioned there?

Write the page. Or re-write the page. No matter what anyone has ever told you, SEO is not about meta tags. Yes, you can include meta tags on your site, and yes, some search engines use them a little bit to determine page content and rank. But most modern search engines like Google and Yahoo use the full-page content plus things like page rank and link text to determine what keywords your page will score well for.

When writing or rewriting your page, keep in mind the following tips to increase your search-engine ranking:

- Include your target phrase at least twice in your page title.
- Include your target phrase twice in the meta description.
- Include your target phrase in the meta keywords.
- Use a header tag to define your page headline, and use your target phrase in that headline.

▶ If you are still determined to use meta tags on your Web site, that is perfectly fine. I use keywords and description on my site to help generate the search-results description and add a few more keywords to my pages. My article "Magic with Meta Tags" (http://about.com/web design/magicwithmeta) should help you build the meta tags that will work best for your Web site.

- Use header tags for your subheads and use your target phrase here too.
- Include your target phrase at least twice in the first paragraph of your Web page.
- If you have relevant images on the page, use the target phrase once in the alt text of the images (making sure that your alt text is still readable and accessible, as described in Chapter 13).
- Sprinkle the target phrase throughout the rest of the document. Put it in links and headlines whenever you can.

I've been writing search-engine optimized Web pages for around eight years now, and even with the benefit of that much experience, the trained writer is likely to cringe at these instructions. It feels like any page written this way will end up being an endless repetition of the keyword phrase with hardly anything else.

But it isn't. This style of writing makes it easier for customers to follow the content. People don't read on the Web the way they read books; they skim. Having a keyword phrase repeated multiple times around a page makes it easier to skim the contents of the page.

Promote the page. Promoting your Web page can be a key way to get it optimized for your target phrase. Make sure you link to it using that phrase, and encourage others to link to it using that phrase as well. Link popularity is one of the secrets to getting better placement in Google. If someone links to your article on cat food with the link text "yummy cat food," and that phrase is picked up by others who also link to your site that way, Google will associate your page with that phrase. This is not the only way that Google determines your page rank, but it is important.

ASK YOUR GUIDE

Should I separate my keywords with commas?

▶ There has been a lot of controversy about this. The argument against says that if you use commas, you're setting up your site to only match on the exact phrase, such as "red dog leashes." But if you don't use commas, you run the risk of having the same word repeated over and over in what appears to be one long keyword phrase, and that repetition can get you penalized. Your best bet is to separate your keywords by commas, not use a lot of keywords, and not worry about it too much. Most search engines don't use the meta keywords for much now anyway.

You mention Google a lot, but shouldn't I be focusing on other search engines too?

▶ It definitely doesn't hurt to focus on other search engines, but if you can get good placement in the most popular search engine, then that will help your placement in other search engines as well. In my article "GaGa for Google" (http://about.com/webdesign/gagagoogle), I provide a number of tips for improving your ranking in Google. The advantage of these tips is that while they're directed at Google, they ultimately end up helping you improve your ranking for every search engine out there.

Check your results and re-optimize. Once you've got a page optimized, your work isn't done. You have to test to make sure that that page's page rank improves.

It can take anywhere from several weeks to several months for the changes you have implemented to take effect in the search engines. I keep a list of the pages I'm working on and check their Google rank every two weeks. The cheapest way to do this is to do a search on Google with your keyword phrase and note where your page appears. You can use a search-engine tracking program to find your page in the results and keep track of it for you.

The challenge with optimizing pages for search engines is that you're never done. Yes, you could argue that getting to the number-one slot in Google for my meta-refresh article is about as far as I can go, but I can't remain complacent. For one thing, Google re-indexes periodically, and when they do that the rankings change, sometimes dramatically. If you had the chance to go behind the scenes at About.com when Google does a re-index, you'd see how hysterical that can make us. Our sites live and die by our placement in search engines, and dropping to page two on Google can mean the difference between chicken ramen or fried chicken for dinner next week.

Avoiding Banishment from Search Engines

Many people believe that SEO is somehow nefarious and that you're tricking the search engines into giving your pages a higher rank. If you follow my instructions you should be fine, as there's nothing nefarious about that style of SEO.

But it is possible to do things that are considered illegal. Depending upon the search engine, those methods can result in anything from a lower rank for that page to a complete ban of all your Web pages in that engine. Many of these are tactics that SEO firms have used in the past, but most have been deemed inappropriate by search-engine operators. Keep in mind, as well, that search-engine companies change their rules all the time. What may be acceptable (or at least unknown) today could become the next automatic-ban offense tomorrow.

When you're optimizing for search engines, always think about the search engine's goal. They want to provide relevant information that their customers are searching for. If a tactic you are using appears to be compromising the relevancy of your information or inflating the value out of proportion to the page, then chances are it will eventually be seen as unacceptable, and you should avoid it. Use common sense, avoid the following tactics, and you should be okay.

Keyword stuffing is a bad idea. Keyword stuffing is the practice of using your keyword so much that it overwhelms the actual content of your Web page. Now, you may be thinking "But she told me to use it twice in the title, twice in the first paragraph, etc." That's true, I did tell you that. But that's not keyword stuffing if you have other content as well. Keyword stuffing looks something like the following. See if you can guess what my target phrase is.

```
<html>
<head>
<title>Dog leashes! Dog leashes! Dog leashes!</
title>
<meta name="keywords" content="dog leashes, big
dog leashes, small dog leashes, expensive dog
leashes, dog leashes for dogs" />
<meta name="description" content="Dog leashes
are important dog apparel. Dog leashes can be
used for every occasion, including taking dog
leashes to dog leash formals and dog leash out-
ings. Your dog leashes will be valuable beyond
the life of your ordinary dog leash and you want
to buy our dog leashes. " />
</head>
<body>
```

ELSEWHERE ON THE WEB

▶ I have been using Position-Pro (www.positionpro.com) for years to track my search-engine optimization. PositionPro helps by analyzing your pages and taking a look at what keywords show up on the page presently. So you can easily compare if your efforts at optimization have made a difference in the eyes of a Web robot. Another good position tracker is the NetMechanic Search Engine Tracker (www.netmechanic.com/products/tracker.shtml).

```
<h1>Dog Leashes</h1>
<h2>Dog Leashes for All Dogs</h2>
<p>Dog leashes. Dog leashes. Dog leashes. Dog
leashes. Dog leashes. Dog leashes. </p>
<p>Get all the dog leashes you could ever want
on this site.</p>
</body>
</html>
```

If you guessed "dog leashes," you are correct. Sure, when the page went live and was spidered by an engine, chances are it would pop to near the top of most keyword-focused search engines. (Google uses algorithms that look at how other sites link to you and is not as focused on keywords.) But it would then be reported by an angry customer of that engine, or, more likely, the engine itself would flag the page as being too keyword heavy and wouldn't rank it at all or would remove it if it had been ranked.

A good rule of thumb is to use your target phrase no more than twice in any one section or element. Be especially careful in the meta data. That is traditionally where keyword stuffing begins because the text doesn't show up on the Web page to the reader. Rather than repeating your keyword phase multiple times, use the keywords to get other phrases that are synonymous onto your page.

Don't hide text from your readers. A few years ago it was a popular tactic to write Web pages with normal content, such as my dog leashes example, but then at the bottom add paragraphs of keyword text that were completely unrelated to the topic but that got a lot of page views (like "sex"). The designer would then hide the text from the readers by adding a font or CSS style to change the color to be the same as the background.

Search engines at the time didn't recognize the text was unreadable and gave the page a higher rank for the keywords used. Doing this today is not only frowned upon, it's easy for the search engine spiders to check, and they do. Remember that while there might be a valid reason for you to write text that is the same color as your background (see my article on building Web Easter eggs at http://about.com/webdesign/hidelinks), most search engines will penalize you if you do it for more than one or two words on a page. The point of Web pages is to impart information, not hide it.

Link farms and free-for-all link pages can hurt your ranking. A link farm is an automated Web site where every item of text on the page is a link. The goal is to increase a site's ranking by adding huge numbers of links to that site, often using the same text.

Free for all (FFA) link pages are similar to link farms, except they allow anyone to post their links on the page. These are some of the most useless sites on the Internet.

Most search engines value relevant links, both on your Web site and to your Web site. FFA and link farms never provide relevant links. They are links for the sake of the <a> tag, and that's a waste of your time. Remember, while Google or Yahoo! might not ban your site today for being on a FFA site, that doesn't mean they won't tomorrow.

Some valid HTML and Web design techniques can also play havoc with search engines. In some ways, search-engine robots are like Web browsers from five or six years ago; they can't read the fancy things that we're putting on our Web pages today. And what a search engine robot can't read, it can't index.

Below is a list of some of the more popular techniques that search engines don't tend to optimize well. That doesn't mean you

WHAT'S HOT

▶ Cloaking is another, more sophisticated way of hiding information. According to Google, cloaking is "a Web site that returns altered Web pages to search engines crawling the site." This means that a human reader coming to your Web site would see different content than the search-engine robot that goes out to spider the Web site. As with changing the text color, you may have a valid reason for cloaking your site, but chances are Google and other search engines will blacklist your site if they find you doing it. For more information on cloaking, read my article "Cloaking: What It Is and Why You Shouldn't Do It" (http://about.com/webdesign/cloaking).

can't use them, but remember that if you're aiming for that number-one spot, these techniques will hurt your ranking:

- **Frames:** Many search engines don't like frames, but if you're going to use them, be sure to include the <noframes> tag with relevant content so that the robots can index your site.
- **Meta refreshes:** These appear to be a cloak, and search engines will penalize sites that use them. Use a 301 permanent redirect instead.
- **Splash pages and Flash:** Search engines are still not good at indexing Flash. If your site starts out with an all-Flash page, the rest of the site won't get indexed. If you must use Flash, provide text links for the search engines to index.
- **Dynamic content:** Dynamic content sites are database driven. They can result in thousands of bogus pages because the search engine increments a number on the end of the URL, and another page appears. Make sure your dynamic pages display errors when incorrect parameters are passed.
- **Ajax and other new technologies:** New technologies may not be accessible. If a technology isn't accessible, then search engines won't like it either.

Other Opportunities for Promotion

Search engine optimization isn't the only way to get your Web pages found by your customers. Promoting a Web site requires the same techniques that any other marketing might require. Ten years ago, it was rare to see a television commercial with a URL listed. Now, if you don't see a URL, you might wonder what's wrong. A lot of promotion techniques are well suited to Web pages, and most of them are not as expensive as television commercials.

Web robots are your friends. You want to create a Web site that welcomes the search-engine robots and makes it easy for them to read and index your Web site. But there's more to it than whether your pages look good to the robots; you also want to make sure your Web site is set up to handle them. Do it with a robots.txt file.

At the root of your Web server is a file called "robots.txt." This file tells the spiders what sections of your site they can and cannot access. There are many reasons why you might not want a robot to access parts of your site. The sections might be private or even access controlled, you might not have a lot of bandwidth, or you might want to only block "Joe's SearchBot" but let the GoogleBot in with unfettered access. My article "Controlling Web Robots" (http://about.com/webdesign/controlwebrobots) explains how to do this.

Submit your site to search engines. But don't oversubmit. Submit your pages no more than once every six to eight weeks. Submitting your site more than that won't get you a better ranking, but it might get you flagged as a spammer and blacklisted.

The best solution for submitting your site is to use "Add URL" pages for the major search engines (you can find many of them on my site at http://about.com/webdesign/addurlpages). There are some good submission services out there, but be wary of companies that either guarantee you a top position or promise to submit your site to thousands of search engines. There is no way to guarantee a top position in the major engines, and any engine that allows you to pay for the top position would be cheaper if you went to it directly. And as for the thousands of submissions, well, there aren't thousands of search engines out there. In many cases, the smaller search engines use the search results of other engines; look for tokens like "Powered by Yahoo!" and the like.

TOOLS YOU NEED

▶ There are many different types of Web robots. Search-engine spiders are one type. My article "What Is a Web Robot?" (http://about.com/webdesign/webrobot) explains what Web robots are and what they are doing on your Web site.

Get a good URL. Some great Web sites out there have been killed because their URL was either too long for customers to remember or it was unprofessional looking. Investing the money in a good domain name is a huge benefit to your marketing and promotion.

Use cheap and free advertising techniques. For example, put your URL on your business cards. When you send out an e-mail message, include your URL in your signature. If you post a relevant comment on a blog, include your site URL, if there's a field for it. If you participate in online forums, include your URL in your signature. In short, mention your URL anywhere you can.

Advertise your Web site. There are many opportunities for advertising, and they fit all budgets. Here are a few ideas:

- Pay-per-click advertising is a great way to pay only what you're willing to pay. The most popular is Google AdWords.
- Banner share programs allow you to advertise on other sites that advertise on yours.
- Get creative. I've seen Web pages advertised on billboards, cars, television and radio, and even on a cow (**www.painted cows.com/specs.html**).

Its simple: Advertising your Web site is a matter of getting the information out to the people who want it.

Get Linked

Promoting Web pages and getting them discovered and highly placed in search engines can be a full-time job in itself. There are a lot of links on my site that can help you move your promotion and SEO efforts to the next level, but I won't promise you number-one ranking.

SEARCH-ENGINE OPTIMIZATION

These links will help you optimize your site, no matter what changes come to search engines.

http://about.com/webdesign/seoptindex

GOOGLE OPTIMIZATION

Google is a very popular search engine, and if you optimize your pages to get good ranking there, half of your promotion work will be done.

http://about.com/webdesign/googleopt

PROMOTION—GETTING MORE PAGE VIEWS

Whether you run a product or a content site, page views will ultimately mean more money. And promotion is how you get people to your site.

http://about.com/webdesign/promoindex

Chapter 11

Making Money with Advertising and E-commerce

How to Make Money on the Web

There are many ways to make money on the Web. Some are more difficult than others. In this chapter, I'll be discussing the following ways to make money from a Web site:

- Pay-per-click advertising
- Banner advertising
- Selling products through e-commerce
- Donations and "shareware" Web sites

Before you can turn on your e-commerce system or place the ads on your site, you need to know who your customers are and what they are looking for. Any site can have ads or e-commerce

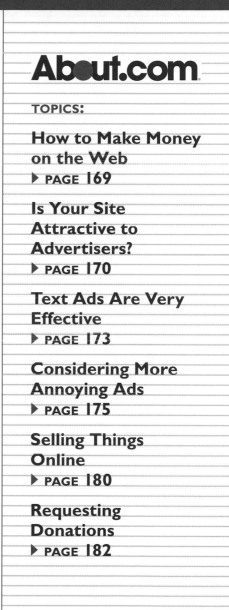

links on it, but you won't sell anything if you aren't linking to products your readers would want.

This is one of the most common mistakes I've seen beginning Web designers make. It can be very tempting to blanket your Web pages with ads and products for sale with no regard to who might buy them or click on them. You may get one or two clicks on these types of pages, but you won't maintain a customer base for very long. People don't come to Web sites to click to other Web sites. They want to get information or products to buy.

If you focus your site on a topic, you'll get readers. When your readers see that you also have related ads or products for sale, they'll be more likely to click on them, and both you and your advertisers will be happy.

Is Your Site Attractive to Advertisers?

There are many ways to make money on the Web, from selling products or services online to creating content that attracts advertising from other companies. In this chapter I'll go over some of the ways you can make money on your Web site and discuss some of the benefits and pitfalls of each method.

Advertising is the first thought that people have when they build a Web site. After all, it sounds pretty easy; simply put up a Web page, and then sell ads on it. But while it sounds easy to do, it can be very difficult to find advertisers who are willing to pay money to put their ads on your Web site.

Do you get enough page views? The most common reason it is difficult to get ads placed on a Web site is because the Web site is too small. The more page views a Web site gets, the more attractive it is to advertisers. If my site gets 100,000 page views a day and yours gets 1,000, advertisers know their ad will be displayed more on my site than on yours.

But page views aren't the only thing. Advertisers also care about how many people see the site. Let's say your site gets 1,000 page views from 1,000 different people. That might make your site more attractive than mine, which is getting 100,000 page views, if I only have 100 people viewing my site. To an advertiser, exposure to 1,000 people might be enough to generate the response they want to that ad.

But that's not all. Even if you have the page views and the visitors, the numbers must be steady. Many Web sites experience a lot of dips and flows in their audience. On About.com, June, July, and August show a huge slump for many sites. Our readers are mostly in the Northern Hemisphere and they apparently take off for the summer to do activities that don't involve surfing the Web (much as we would like them to). But some Web sites see fluctuations that are even more random. Say you got "slashdotted," meaning that the popular technology site, Slashdot (<u>http://slashdot.</u><u>org</u>), linked to you and may have even crashed your site because of the increase in hits. Your site might get a million page views in that week. While that is great, you can't then take those numbers to an advertiser and say "I get 1 million page views per week."

Don't forget niche markets. Even if your site doesn't get the page views that a major advertiser might want, if you have a targeted, niche market for your site, you might be able to get targeted, niche advertisers. For example, there may not be a lot of people who are passionately interested in model airplanes, but existing fans are extremely interested. If your site focuses on model airplanes, you could get dealers and stores to advertise on your site. The benefit to them is they get a targeted audience and a less expensive ad than on a site that gets a million page views a week. The benefit to you is obvious: money.

But in order to be attractive to these advertisers, you need to make sure that your topic is appropriate to their niche. You also want to make sure that when people search for items in your topic, your page appears near the top of the results. Advertisers are people just like you and me, and they search the Web too. If they see a site that is writing for their audience, they'll want to advertise with you. But they won't come to you.

Provide information that advertisers can use. Selling advertising space is very much like selling a product—you need to hook the customer, show them what you have to offer, provide them with the pricing, and then make it easy for them to buy. If you're selling ads on your Web site, include the following information:

- **The demographics of your readers:** Advertisers want to know that they are advertising on a site that serves the people they want to target.
- **Page views, including the number of unique visitors:** You wouldn't buy a car without knowing its gas mileage. Why would you expect your advertisers to buy without knowing your site statistics?
- **Rules about the banners you display:** If you have size or content restrictions, state that clearly in your guidelines.
- **Where you display the ads and how long they remain:** This can affect the price. A banner displayed in a prominent spot on your home page might be worth more than a small icon placed somewhere else.
- **How much it costs to advertise on your site:** This is defined in the price per thousand impressions (called PPM).

Make it easy for advertisers. The easier you make anything, the more likely your target audience will do it. And the best way to make advertising easy is to use advertising software or an advertising agency to handle your advertising. Advertising software helps you place ads on your Web site and then track them for your customers. Some of the more sophisticated programs work with you on your reporting and help manage all aspects of advertising on a Web site.

Having software that will do the work for you is one thing, but an advertising agency can mean the difference between getting the ad and not. Advertising agencies work with companies to help build ads for Web sites, and they also work with companies to place those ads on sites. The About.com Guide to Advertising lists a lot of Web advertising agencies that are exclusively devoted to advertising on the Internet (http://about.com/advertising/agencies).

Text Ads Are Very Effective

These days, the most common type of advertisement you'll see on the Web is a text ad. It has been shown that these ads are more effective at selling product and generating click-through than the traditional banner ad. Text ads are usually what is called pay-per-click (PPC) and they are generated by automated systems to relate to keywords on your Web site. They are the easiest way to get advertising on your Web site because all you need to do is insert some JavaScript code onto your pages and the ads appear.

Pay-per-click advertising is more cost effective. Advertisers like PPC ads because they are more cost effective. Instead of paying for impressions (the number of times the ad is seen by someone), they pay only when the ad is clicked on. And since most people only click on things that are interesting to them, they are more likely to buy after they've clicked that link.

Most PPC engines allow advertisers to do the following things to modify several variables to affect how their ad displays:

TOOLS YOU NEED

▶ There are hundreds of advertising software tools available on the Web. Finding one that works for you can be very difficult. The "Advertising Software" category on my About.com site (http://about.com/webdesign/advsoft) lists some of the available software packages you can use to manage ads on your Web site.

- Choose specific keywords to target so that the ad shows on pages that apply to the topic.
- Choose how much they're willing to pay per click.
- Change how often the ad is displayed.
- Decide how much total money will be spent on a campaign.

When an advertiser targets a keyword or keyword phrase that your site is optimized for, that ad is more likely to show up on your Web site. This benefits both of you: It helps improve your keyword ranking and keeps your customers happy. Your page appears more professional because it has ads that relate to your topic.

When an advertiser indicates how much she will spend per click on an ad to specific keywords, that determines how valuable your site is. For example, if you have written an article about dogs, and today the keyword "dogs" is selling for $10 per click, your site would have more value than a site targeting some other keyword that sells for less.

I'm not suggesting that you go out and find the most expensive keywords and then write a site on that. Instead, focus on getting as many page views as you can for the topic you know well. Then, even if your PPC rate is only around 10 cents, you'll still make money. Everyone is focusing on the $10-per-click keywords, but if you stick to the medium-priced keywords, you'll be better able to get the ads on your site. And having the targeted ads will help your ranking so you'll get more page views so you'll get more clicks on your ads.

One of the drawbacks to a site that gets a lot of page views is you can drive your ads off your site. Many of the keywords that have large dollar amounts per click have low total value for the ad campaign. In other words, an advertiser with a budget of $100 will run out of money after ten clicks on a $10-per-click ad. Once the money is gone, so is the ad.

ELSEWHERE ON THE WEB

▶ One of the most popular and best-known pay-per-click solutions is Google AdWords (https://adwords.google.com/select/Login) for advertisers to advertise their sites and AdSense (https://www.google.com/adsense) for Web page designers to host ads on their sites. If you're looking to host text ads on your site, I would start with AdSense. It's easy to use, and people are very familiar with the ads it creates.

Text ads are perceived better by your customers. While there are definitely people who don't like advertisements of any type, most customers prefer to read text ads over banners and large graphical treatments. This is not to say that text ads get better results for the advertisers, but only that your customers will like them better.

The nice thing about text ads is that they are better targeted than a banner ad campaign. This is because banner ads are much more expensive to run, so there are ads called "run of network" or generic ads. In banner exchanges, you'll see these as the banners that are advertising the banner exchange. You'll even see these on television, when the station advertises another show on the same channel or network. While these ads are useful, an actual paid ad makes the company more money, and they will always want to replace generic ads with paying ads.

Most PPC companies don't have generic ads (other than the standard "Ads by [company]" link at the top of the ad block). Instead, when there are no ads for the keyword, no ads are displayed. This doesn't happen very often. After all, the PPC company is paid to display clickable ads. They don't benefit from empty ad blocks any more than you do.

Considering More Annoying Ads

While text ads are most preferred by customers, the pop-up, pop-under, slide-in, take-over-your-screen annoying banner ads are preferred by advertisers. They are preferred because they work at getting the attention the advertisers are looking for. And they are willing to pay for them. If your site is getting big enough, text ads may not be enough to pay the bills, and you'll want to look at other ad styles. There are a number of them:

- **Banner ads:** These are the standard graphical banners you see on many Web sites. They are typically 468 × 60 pixels and are found on the top of pages and at the bottom. They can be animated or flat images, but they usually don't have any special effects like Flash.
- **Skyscraper or tower ads:** These are tall and thin ads. They are very similar to banner ads except that they run vertically on Web pages and are found in the left and right columns of sites.
- **Square ads:** They are usually 336 × 280 pixels in size (so not exactly square) and usually live within the content of a Web page. Content flows around the ad. (About.com Guides refer to these as "BHA" (big, honking ads), but I don't think that's the accepted terminology.)
- **Pop-ups:** If you don't know what these are, you've never browsed the Web or only started browsing a year or two ago with Firefox. These ads open in a new window, and are usually generated with a script like JavaScript.
- **Pop-under ads:** These are similar to pop-ups, but rather than appearing above the window you're looking at, they appear below it. Advertisers seem to like them because people don't always realize that they've opened, and so don't close them as quickly.
- **Interstitial ads:** These are ads that open when you click on a link. You can tell you've gotten an interstitial ad because there will be a "go on to content" or skip link.
- **Rich media ads:** These can appear in any of the above styles of ads, but they are more than just images—they are Flash and provide more interaction with the ad right on the page.
- **Overlays (also called eyeblasters or shoshkeles):** These use Flash to place the advertising right on the page you're on. They typically slide into view on top of any content on the

page, and you have to click a close button or wait for them to finish before they'll go away.

There are many benefits to these types of ads. While most of the benefits are to you rather than to your customer, they can mean the difference between your site staying in business or not.

The more annoying ads have a higher click-through rate than more standard ads. Unlike other types of advertising, like television and radio, Web ads are paid for based upon very measurable pieces of data: either how many times the ad was viewed or how many times the ad was clicked on. A company advertising on your Web site wants to make sure that its ad will be seen by the people who will act on the ad, will be seen often enough to promote familiarity and trust, and will be clicked on.

The more interesting the ad, the more likely it is to be clicked on. Ads like eyeblasters and shoshkeles are clicked on more because they are more exciting and visually appealing. One reason people may be clicking on them is because they cover content, and people click on them to make them go away.

Even pop-up ads get a better click-through rate than standard banner ads. Many eye-tracking studies have found that people don't see the ads at the top or sides of the page. One of the only places on a page that banner ads get good traffic is at the bottom of the page. If a customer has read the entire page, he is ready to click on an advertisement.

Many sites use rich media ads (like eye-blasters) as a way to reinforce their brand. In some cases, it doesn't even matter if the ad is clicked on. The goal of these ads is to increase awareness. I have seen this used a lot with movies. An overlay ad is placed on related sites that promote the movie. It is possible to click on the ad and go to the movie Web site, but that doesn't really matter to the advertiser. What the movie company wants you to do is go to the theater and see the film. Clicking through to their movie Web site might make them some money, but their real money comes from ticket sales and DVD sales later. That means they need to brand their ads so that you recognize the film later as something you wanted to see.

Rich media ads cost more than text or banner ads, but because they generate more interest and click-through, they are more cost effective. There are now more Flash designers out there who can build the rich media ads, so the cost to develop the ads is coming down, which make them even more cost effective.

But rich media ads aren't beneficial just to the advertiser; they can be beneficial to your customers, too. Rich media ads are more interesting and fun to view than their more boring banner and text counterparts. I don't like having my screen taken over by an advertisement, but when it's a cool overlay of Johnny Depp advertising his new movie, I don't mind as much. The challenge for most Web-page owners is that someone else has control over the ad content. As rich media ads get more popular with advertisers, the quality will go down and this benefit will be reduced.

There are also many drawbacks to intrusive ads. One of the most obvious is that many people hate them. I've found that if you ask someone what she thinks of online advertising, she will instantly tell you she hates it, and then tell a story of the most annoying ad she's ever seen. But what is so awful about them? After all, some ads we like. For example, most people can remember seeing or at least hearing about the Mac 1984-style ad that came out in the 1980s: http://en.wikipedia.org/wiki/1984_(television_commercial). While not all ads on Web sites are of that caliber, some are at least interesting or fun to read or watch.

Most people hate ads that take over the Web site. Most people respond very negatively to takeover ads. I question the validity of the click-through rates on these ads as it can be hard to make them go away; I have clicked on many takeover ads in my effort to get back to the page that I wanted.

Ads that launch audio (or video with audio) are also very annoying. These ads don't take into account that most of us are already surrounded by sounds we have chosen. When an ad starts talking or making music, it is disruptive and can overpower the ambient music we are listening to. In some cases it can even get people in trouble if they are browsing at work. I find the ads that make noise when you mouse over them especially annoying. There was an ad on my About.com site that would start talking in a computer-generated voice whenever you moved your mouse across it. Since the ad was either in the banner at the top or a tower on the right, I was rolling my mouse over it all the time. I got to the point that if I saw that ad loading on my site, I would refresh the page until it was gone rather than risk listening to it at random.

One thing to remember when you are selling ads on your site is that customers don't usually associate the annoying ad with the advertiser: They associate it with you. This is the biggest drawback to annoying advertisements. A new customer might be driven away from my site, never to return, because some over-eager advertising manager placed an annoying ad on my site.

It is very rare that you will hear someone say, "I won't buy X product because those ads are annoying." But I have gotten loads of e-mails saying, "I will never come back to your Web site because of the annoying ads." It's important to make money from your Web site, but if you don't have any customers, you won't make any money anyway. Try to strike a balance.

ELSEWHERE ON THE WEB

▶ It's not just the ads that people hate, but the way they are presented. In a study done by Jakob Nielsen (www.useit.com/alertbox/20041206.html) pop-ups were the most hated, but ads that load slowly or try to trick you into clicking on them were nearly as unpopular. Ads that play audio, blink on and off, or don't have a close button are equally annoying.

▶ Forms are one of the trickiest items on a Web site, but you can learn how to build them quicker than you might think. My Free HTML Forms class (http://about.com/webdesign/html formscourse) teaches you the basics of building Web forms and goes into how to set up scripts on the server to use the forms.

Selling Things Online

Another way to make money on a Web site is by selling products or services online. In Chapter 6 I covered the details of building a product Web page. That is the first step, but after you have a product page, you need to have a way to sell those products.

Do you need a shopping cart or storefront? If you are only selling one or two items, a shopping cart or storefront may be overkill. In this situation, it's easier to set up a simple order form for your customers to order the item.

Remember that even if you're going to have a simple order form, you must make it secure. This means that you should use a server that can support secure Web sites (http://about.com/web design/secureservers) and have SSL turned on on that server so that all transactions are encrypted.

Shopping carts work within your existing Web site. Shopping carts work well when you don't have a lot of products to sell and have a Web site built. But they require some knowledge of HTML and some type of programming engine on your Web server (like PHP, Perl, or Python). Some shopping carts are hosted on another Web server, but that moves into the realm of storefront.

When you set up a shopping cart, there are a few things you need to think about before you can start selling:

- **Secure servers are very important to online shoppers.** If you can't offer the https and the lock icon in the browser window, your customers won't want to purchase from you.
- **Will you accept credit cards or other methods of payment?** The easier you make it for your customers the more likely you'll make a sale, but the more methods of payment you offer, the more expensive it will be to build and maintain.

- **You need to know how you're going to deliver the goods.** If you're selling products, include shipping and handling fees. It's also nice to have your site integrated with a shipping provider like FedEx or UPS. If you're selling downloadable products, you need to be able to deliver those as well.
- **Taxes are always an issue.** Many states in the United States are taxing online sales regardless of where the sale is made or shipped to. A shopping cart tool that assists in handling taxes can be very helpful.

Shopping carts require less work on your part than storefronts because they are more integrated into your Web site. Make sure that the shopping cart is easy to use and that there isn't anything blocking the sale. But even with hosted shopping carts, the most interaction your customers will have with it is to verify their order and submit their purchasing information. As long as that is easy to do and runs quickly, the shopping cart should work out fine.

Using a storefront or hosted shopping-cart site can make online stores easy to set up. Sites like Amazon, eBay, and Yahoo! all offer online storefronts for small businesses. The benefit to these types of Web sites is that they have a strong brand associated with security and online sales. When you attach your storefront to these sites, your customers won't be worried about putting their credit card into your form because chances are they'll be customers of the parent site.

Storefront partnerships make it easy to start selling online because they handle all the difficult parts. Your store will accept different payment methods and possibly even other currencies; plus, you'll get a lot of metrics to track your store and how you're doing. You may also get some promotion from within the parent

It's so hard to decide what shopping cart or storefront to use. What tools do you recommend?

▶ A Google search for "shopping cart" returns millions of pages. Finding a shopping cart that works well for what you need can be tough. When I set up shopping carts, I find it helps to find an all-encompassing solution rather than trying to do it myself. I prefer sites like Yahoo! Stores (http://small business.yahoo.com/ecom merce) and eBay (http:// pages.ebay.com/storefronts/ start.html) because they make it easy for you to set up a safe and secure store-front.

site (not a lot, so don't rely on this). And most allow you to create your storefront so that it looks just like your existing site.

When you're building your online storefront, make sure that it's as easy to use as the rest of your Web site. Because most storefronts are hosted on a different server, you should be very aware of things like the size of your images and where they are hosted so that your customers aren't frustrated by slow load times or even missing images.

Requesting Donations

Another way you can make money on a Web site is by asking for it. While it is true that most people would like to have something for nothing, many also realize that most of us are not independently wealthy. Content providers need some money to keep providing the articles, information, or services that they've come to enjoy.

Readers care about themselves, not you. No one would say that it was possible to create a product and give it away forever. But most people don't make the leap from there to thinking "I like this Web site. How can I help it stay in business?" Therefore, you need to make sure that your readers and potential donors understand how donating benefits them.

People are more willing to donate their time than their money. One way you can get help for your site is by requesting donations of that time. Make it easy for them to add what you'd like to see added.

I can tell you from first-hand experience that this works. On my About.com Web Design/HTML site, I have put out requests for articles and reviews. I have even offered payment for these items. The only responses I would get were either spam or so poorly written I couldn't use them. But when About.com added comments to our blog posts, I started getting a lot of interesting content.

While new content is not cash, the concept is the same. Make it as easy as possible for your readers to become contributors. And provide some benefit to those people who do donate. Perhaps they see the newsletter a day sooner than everyone else, maybe they get access to the private blogs by your CEO, or maybe there's a forum just for members. It doesn't have to be a lot, but providing a benefit for donating is important. On one site I read, a donation of $5 gets you a star icon next to your name in the forums for a month. It's easy for people to do, and they obviously like it because they donate the $5 every month.

Micropayments may be unpopular, but they work. Micropayments are tiny charges for elements in a program or on a Web site. The problem with micropayments is that they are misused. Customers don't like it when they have to pay 10 cents for every article they read on your site, especially if they have to pay it every time they come. This reaction is similar to sites that require a login to read the articles. Many people refuse to log in, even if it's free.

When micropayments work, they work because they are adding something to the site, game, or program, not blocking that site, game, or program. For example, if you have an online game, you want people to come play it. You could make the game free or even charge for initial access to it. Where micropayments come in is in buying extras for the game. But users are not prevented from participating if they don't want to pay.

It can't hurt to ask, can it? Paypal (www.paypal.com) has a simple form you can fill out to accept donations on your Web site. If you ask for donations and no one gives you any, you're no worse off than you were before. Be careful that you don't imply that your information or products are somehow inferior. Make the request for a donation look classy and integrated into your Web site.

Get Linked

Making money on Web sites is difficult. There are a lot of people competing for the same money you're after. These links will give you more information to help you make money on your Web site.

ADVERTISING ON THE WEB

If you're trying to make money through ads, learn how to create effective Web ads and how to use them well.

http://about.com/webdesign/advertising

WEB SERVERS

If you're going to host your own shopping cart, you'll need to make sure that you have a Web server that can handle your needs. These links and articles will teach you more about Web servers and using them effectively.

http://about.com/webdesign/webservers

Chapter 12

Optimizing Your Site for Speed

Keep Your Customers' Connection in Mind

Nearly every Web designer I know builds her Web sites using some form of high-speed Internet: cable modem, **DSL**, fractional-T1, or full-**T1**. In order to do our jobs, we need high-speed access to transfer files quickly and get our pages up for testing and review. But while we may have high-speed access, our customers may not.

You test in different browsers, but do you test on a dial-up connection? One day I was staying at my parents' house, and I had to connect to our company site to fix something. My parents didn't have high-speed access, so I was forced to use a dial-up connection. I connected to our home page and was shocked at how slowly it loaded. We had done evaluations and used tools to tell us how long it would take to download, and yet when I tried it out, it was almost physically painful.

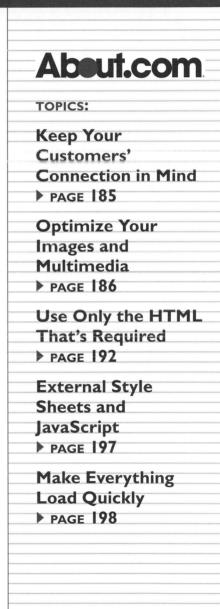

About.com

Seven to ten seconds is all the time you have. It's important to have a page that loads as quickly as possible. But before you start optimizing for that amount of time, test your pages to see how fast they load. Seven seconds is a fairly long time to wait for most Web pages. If your home page is in the ten-second range, it's pushing the upper limit of what people will wait for.

Here are the basics of Web site optimization:

- Create small images that download quickly.
- Use only the HTML that you need to get your point across.
- Use external resources whenever possible.
- Minimize the white space in your HTML code.
- Ensure that any external content also loads quickly.

Optimize Your Images and Multimedia

Images and multimedia are the biggest sources of long download times. If you do nothing else, make sure that your images, Flash, and sound files are as small as you can possibly make them.

The most important thing to remember when adjusting images and multimedia file sizes is that you can't do it with a Web browser or HTML editor. For example, if you have an image that is 4000 × 4000 pixels in size, the Web browser can resize it by changing the height and width in the HTML like this:

```
<img src="bigimage.gif" height="400" width="400"
alt="big image" />
```

The image will display in the browser as if it were only 400 × 400 pixels. But the download time will be the same as if it were displayed at 4000 × 4000 pixels because it's the same file. Always use a graphics editor to resize your images so that the file size and dimensions are small.

TOOLS YOU NEED

▶ If you're learning to optimize your Web site for speed, my article series "Web Site Optimization: Build Web Pages That Download Fast" (http://about.com/webdesign/siteopt) offers hints for improving your site and making it download more quickly.

The easiest way to optimize images and multimedia is to not use them at all. It can be very tempting to use images for everything on a Web page. If you use an image, you know it will look the same no matter who views the page. But pages that are built completely in images and Flash are a lot slower to download than similar HTML and text pages. Plus, search engines can't index the text in images and have a hard time reading Flash. So a site that is all multimedia and no text is not going to rank as high in search engines as one that isn't.

Here are a few situations where using text, CSS, or HTML results in a page that looks just as good but downloads a lot faster:

- **Don't use graphics for textual headlines.** Use CSS instead. It is possible to create CSS headlines that look just as good as the graphical alternative, and you'll be optimized for search engines as well as download speed.
- **Don't use graphical lines.** It can be very tempting to dress up a Web page with graphical lines. But unless there is a very complex graphical element to the line, you can usually duplicate it with CSS on <hr/> tags or border properties on your elements.
- **Curvy corners don't require images.** You can use CSS to create rounded edges on many elements of Web pages. I explain how on my Web site (**http://about.com/webdesign/rounded**).
- **Images for drop caps are not required.** Use CSS. There's even a CSS pseudo-element for drop caps (**http://about.com/webdesign/cssdropcaps**).
- **Don't use spacer GIFs.** Instead of spacer GIF files, use CSS padding and margin properties to adjust where you want your elements to display (**http://about.com/webdesign/paddingmargin**).

Remember, graphics can improve your Web page, but too many can ruin it. Some of the most popular sites on the Web, such as Google, use almost no graphics at all.

Use the correct image type to keep the file size small. There are five standard image types that are used on Web pages: GIF, JPEG, **PNG**, JP2, and SVG. There are reasons to use each type, and using the wrong type will make your images download more slowly.

The GIF format is used when your images have a limited number of colors. I like to think of them as the cartoons of Web pages because they are not photo-realistic. A GIF file can have a maximum of 256 colors, and smaller GIF files use fewer colors. Use GIF files for the following:

- Logos
- Icons
- Simple animation
- Images that need to have a transparent area

JPEG or JPG files are used for images with millions of colors, like photographs or gradients. Always save photographs as JPEGs because the colors will be remain closer to the original. JPEGs use a compression algorithm that makes them smaller than when saved as a GIF. Use JPEG files for the following:

- Photographs
- Gradients
- Complicated or faded background images

The PNG (for portable network graphic) format was designed as an alternative to GIF and JPEG files. PNG files handle images with millions of colors as well as they do images with flat color palettes. But PNG offers some additional features that GIF and JPEG files do not:

- PNG files have a better compression rate than GIFs. If you save the same file as a GIF or a PNG, the PNG will be between 5 and 25 percent smaller.
- PNG files use lossless compression, unlike JPEG. When you resize a file as a JPEG, data may be lost. When you save a photograph as a PNG, all the data remains in the file.
- Alpha transparency creates variable transparent areas. With a GIF file you can create a transparent section of your image, but it is 100 percent transparent. PNG files allow you to display images that have a variable transparency, adding tints to the image, depending where it's placed on the page.

While you can use PNG files for photographs, always check the image quality and the file size compared to the JPEG format. Use PNG files where you would have used GIF files to take advantage of the better compression. Use GIF files only for animations.

JP2 or JPEG 2000 is a new graphics format that offers lossy and lossless compression for photographic images. This results in much smaller files than standard JPEG files. The problem is that most popular browsers still don't support JP2 files.

SVG (scalable vector graphics) is based on XML. SVG files are very flexible for changing size (scalability) and programming. The images are very compact, and they are becoming popular on mobile devices. SVG files are only supported in some browsers.

Multimedia files benefit from using the right format as well. When creating a sound file for your Web site, you have the option of using MP3, WAV, or even AUD files. MP3 files are smaller than the other formats, but they are not always supported in the Web browser. MP3 files are best suited for podcasts and other applications where you expect your listeners to want high-quality sound and be willing to use an external program to hear it. If you want to have sound play while your customers are on your Web site, use the WAV or AUD formats. As with images, save the file in multiple formats to determine if you have the best quality and smallest size you can achieve.

Flash is popular for video files, but you can also save your files as MPEG, WMV, or QuickTime. The advantage to using Flash is that nearly every Web browser has the Flash plugin, and it's not operating system dependant like QuickTime (which plays on both Windows and Macintosh but is considered a Macintosh product) or WMV (Windows only).

Crop out what isn't needed. When you're optimizing your images, be sure to crop them so that they are as small as possible. This brings what's important into focus.

While cropping refers to images, consider doing a similar thing to your sound and video files. Edit Web video to include only the scenes that are required to get the message across. Many beginning filmmakers don't want to leave anything out, but editing your video makes it tighter and helps it download faster.

The same is true for sound files. Unless you are doing live broadcasting on your Web site, most sound files can be edited and still retain the sense of the interview or sound clip. If it's an interview, include the introduction as text on the associated Web page. If it's a music file, chances are you need just a short segment rather than the entire song.

There are also tricks specific to the file format. When you're optimizing a JPEG file, be aware that JPEGs compress blurred areas more than crisper areas. You can use this to your advan-

▶ I don't like Web sites that embed sound on the pages, but in some situations it makes sense. If you want to learn how to include sound on your Web pages, read my article "Learn How to Include Sound on Your Web Pages" (http://about.com/ webdesign/sound). You'll learn about the two tags you can use and how and when to use them.

tage when optimizing JPEGs. Mask the most important part of the image, and then apply a very light blur to the background. This will make the important part of the image stand out, and the JPEG will save as a smaller file than with a sharp background.

GIF and PNG files use color indexes to indicate which colors will be used in the image. When optimizing these file types, reduce the number of colors to the minimum required to create the image. The trick here is that most graphics programs default to a large number of colors in the index, something like 256. If your graphic only has three colors, 253 other colors in the index increase the file size. Make sure to save your GIF and PNG files with only the colors you're using.

Another trick with GIF and PNG files is to avoid vertical lines. Because of the way the compression algorithm works, if your image has mostly vertical bands of color, it will be larger than a similar image with mostly horizontal bands of color. In this online example, the image with vertical lines is three times larger (**http://about.com/webdesign/gifopt**).

Dithering is another space hog when it comes to GIF and PNG files. Dithering allows you to create images with gradients, but it vastly increases the file size. Here's a test that shows the differences in file sizes when you save a file with dithering and without: (**http://about.com/webdesign/giftest**). If you must save a file as a GIF with a gradient, be sure to test all your options to make your file as small as possible.

Animated GIFs add more complexity to optimization, but it is possible to make them quite small if you work at it. If you are using a lot of animated GIFs, invest in a high-quality graphics software tool like Fireworks or ImageReady. The tool will take a lot of the optimization tasks out of your hands and create smaller GIFs for you. When creating animated GIFs, keep these things in mind:

TOOLS YOU NEED

▶ Flash files can get big if you're not careful. But there are ways to optimize them so that they remain as small as possible. Always optimize the fonts you use (http://about .com/webdesign/fontsopt) and learn how to optimize the shapes in your file (http:// about.com/webdesign/shape sopt). Flash has a built-in optimizer, but it only works if you know how to use it.

- Follow all the instructions for creating optimized GIF files, including cropping, color management, and so on.
- Use the same colors from frame to frame. The fewer changes you make, the smaller your file will be.
- Avoid using redundant frames. As with video, you don't want to have extra frames if you don't need them.

There's one last trick for improving download times of images. Always define the height and width of the image for the Web browser. You can define this in the image tag itself or in CSS identifiers for each image. While this won't change the download time for the image, it speeds up the rendering time for the Web browser, as it doesn't have to figure out what the image height and width are.

Use Only the HTML That's Required

Optimizing Web pages for speed isn't just about images and multimedia; it's also about the HTML that you have on the page. Many Web pages use more HTML than is required to create the page. Getting rid of extraneous tags and reordering the elements you keep will help your Web page load as fast as possible.

First, look at your content length. That can be the easiest thing to reduce because it doesn't require a change to your page design or HTML. Pages that are really long take more time to download.

You have to balance download time with site usability. People are more likely to scroll in a Web page when they realize that there is something to scroll for. It is easier to read a long Web document by scrolling down than to click through several screens of text. This is because you don't lose your mental context when scrolling, but the act of clicking will cause that context to disappear. The other benefit to longer pages is that they are easier to skim, which is how people read on the Web.

If you need to write 3,000 words to get your point across, then you should write that much. But if 2,000 of those words are redundant, get rid of them. Editing content for a Web page should be just as ruthless as for print. As Strunk and White say in their *Elements of Style*, "Vigorous writing is concise. A sentence should contain no unnecessary words, a paragraph no unnecessary sentences, for the same reason that a drawing should have no unnecessary lines and a machine no unnecessary parts." Make every word in your Web page count.

Don't use redundant HTML. Extra HTML tags that you think are needed for layout or design can bog down even the smallest page. Following are some of the most commonly overused tags with advice on how to get rid of them.

Font tags should be completely abolished in favor of CSS. If you've been building your Web page from this book, you haven't used font tags. Those of you who still use font tags are wasting download time. With CSS, you can define the exact fonts you need for your entire document with one line (**http://about .com/webdesign/usecss**), and then use style classes or IDs to define exceptions (**http://about.com/webdesign/styleclassesids**).

The <div> tag is also overused on modern Web sites. The problem comes from Web templates. Since the template builders don't know what content you're going to have in the section, they create it with a <div> rather than a header, list, or other block level element. Think semantically when you build your pages, and use tags that reflect what the content is rather than where it lives on the page. Another thing I see a lot is a <div> with an ID surrounding another block level element like an <h1>. Instead of using the extra <div>, why not put the ID on the <h1>? You can read more about how to avoid "divitis" online as well (**http://about.com/web-design/divoveruse**).

▶ When you build a Web
page, you're building it in three
parts: the structure (HTML),
the style (CSS), and the behaviors (JavaScript). Building a
semantic Web-page means
that you look at the content
and have the structure define
that. For example, with CSS
we can define a Web-page
header as red, bold, and
1.5ems. To get that look, it
doesn't matter whether we
can use a <div>, a <p>, or a
<h1> tag. But because the
content is supposed to be a
header, we must use the <h1>
to be semantically correct.
In my article "What Is the
Semantic Web?" (http://about.
com/webdesign/semanticweb),

Nested tables cause HTML tag bloat. Nesting tables takes Web browsers longer to render than a similar sized page that doesn't have nested tables. Keep your tables simple and your pages will load faster.

Frames slow your Web page down because there is more to download. If you have a Web page that has two frames, there will be three HTML documents for the browser to request and download—one for each frame and one for the frameset definition. The only way to get around this is not to use frames.

Another place that Web pages get bloated is comments. Comments tell the developers how the page is built and make it easier to maintain. If you're serious about creating the smallest page you can, delete the comments from your pages.

Even white space can make a difference in page download times. Every byte counts. If your hosting provider charges for bandwidth, extra white space can have a huge impact on your site costs. If you have thousands or millions of pages, each byte can add up very quickly.

Check to see if you have a lot of extra white space in your HTML:

1. Open your Web page in a Web browser.
2. View the source of your Web page.
3. Check for the following:
   Indenting
   Multiple carriage returns between elements
   Extra spaces between words or tags

Indenting is nice when you need to edit the code by hand, because it makes the content easier to read. But it can get out of hand, especially if you tend to indent (and move to a new line) any new HTML tag. Multiple carriage returns are usually added by programs building Web pages automatically. Another place you might see extra carriage returns is when you use include files. A carriage return before and after the include statement as well as in the included file all add up quickly. And extra spaces between words don't show up on the page, but they have to be downloaded.

White space can appear without your realizing it, especially if you use a server technology like JSP or PHP to build your pages. Once I saw a database-driven Web site where the actual HTML didn't start for fifty lines. The first fifty lines of the document were all JSP code that wasn't rendered by the Web browser; instead, the server passed along a carriage return for every line of JSP. Fifty carriage returns might not seem like a lot, but this was for a home page that received 50,000 page views a day. Fifty bytes times 50,000 is a lot of bandwidth just for carriage returns. If you use server code like PHP, ASP, or JSP, make sure that it doesn't add in additional characters to your Web page.

Order your document so that the important things load first. Once you've gotten rid of the extra content and tags, take a look at the structure of your Web document. Whenever possible, put the most important elements of your Web page at the top. Web browsers read HTML documents from top to bottom, and they attempt to begin rendering the page as soon as possible. If you place interesting content near the top, your customers will be more likely to stick around reading that content while the rest of the page loads. This is called progressive downloading.

If you have multimedia content on your Web page, make sure that there is something else on the page to keep your customers engaged while they are waiting for the item to download. Don't assume that your content is so interesting that they will wait for it.

ELSEWHERE ON THE WEB

▶ If you are interested in creating a Web page that downloads as quickly as possible, consider learning extreme HTML optimization, or EHO. EHO is a set of guidelines to help you create the leanest functioning HTML code possible. Some of the recommendations violate XHTML and HTML standards, but if speed is more important, then do what you need to do. The basic tips are listed in the article "Extreme HTML Optimization" (www.webreference .com/authoring/languages/ html/optimize/8.html).

Elements like layers and image maps should be placed as close to the closing body tag as possible without destroying the Web page. Many browsers don't understand layers and so ignore them anyway.

Keep your invisible content as short as possible. Every Web page has content that isn't visible to the average reader. Things like CSS hooks (ID attributes and classes), file names, and meta data all are required on your Web page and take up space in the download. Here are some ways to make your hidden data download faster:

- Use short file names, class names, and IDs.
- Keep meta titles, keywords, and descriptions short.
- Use relative path image and link URLs.

A relative path URL defines a URL that is on the same domain as the current page. So you can leave off both the identifier and the domain and still reach the file or image. You can only link to pages on your own server this way. I could link to a URL with an anchor tag like this: `<a href="/od/beginningtutorials/a/aa040502a.htm">`.

You can speed up other documents by how you link to them. Pay attention to how you link to other Web pages.

Always include the trailing slash on URLs. When you leave them off, the Web server has to do two checks: one to determine if it's looking for a file or a directory and a second to determine which file to display. The trailing slash tells the server it's a directory so it knows to look for the default file.

If possible, include the file name you want to link to rather than relying on the default server name. So, instead of linking to http://webdesign.about.com or http://webdesign.about .com/, link to http://webdesign.about.com/index.htm. This tells the Web server exactly what file it should deliver.

I don't recommend writing invalid XHTML. Some proponents of EHO recommend doing things like removing all quote marks and closing tags. While this will save some space in your Web pages, it will also guarantee that your Web pages won't validate as XHTML. If your pages aren't written correctly, you can't be sure how a Web browser will render the page.

Also, CSS relies on the closing tags to know where to apply and stop applying styles to your elements. If you don't have closing tags, then your document tree will be incorrect and your CSS won't work as expected.

Both closing tags and quoted attributes are required elements of valid XHTML. Removing them for the sake of download speed is not a good idea.

External Style Sheets and JavaScript

Style sheets and JavaScript take up space on your Web pages, and they do contribute to the download times. But you need to style your pages and provide behaviors.

Use external CSS files. External CSS files are stored outside of your HTML document and then referenced in the head of your HTML.

External style sheets are very useful for Web sites because they collect all the styles in one place. If every page on your Web site references the same style sheet, you can change your whole site at once and take advantage of caching as well. This means that after your reader downloads the style sheet the first time, her browser won't need to download it for any subsequent pages she reads.

Use only one CSS file for your site. The more linked or imported style sheets you have in a document, the more the server requests are sent to build the document. If you are trying to optimize your Web site for download speed, consider collapsing your CSS files into one large style sheet. The fewer requests to the server, the faster your page will load.

Use external script files. External scripts are similar to CSS files. If you have one JavaScript file that you reference in all your Web pages, you can take advantage of caching for faster downloads. The About .com Guide to JavaScript has an excellent article explaining how to write external scripts (**http://about.com/javascript/learnjavascript**).

If you don't want to use external scripts, or if they must be loaded in the body of your document, place them as close to the ending body tag as possible. This ensures that the content loads first, giving your readers a chance to see what's on the page.

Make Everything Load Quickly

The key to Web-page optimization is to make everything load as quickly as you can. In order to do that, you need to use the smallest tags, style properties, and scripts; use fewer images; make fewer calls to the Web server; and make sure your externally loaded elements load quickly, too.

Use shorthand CSS tags to speed up style sheets. Shorthand CSS styles are style properties that condense multiple styles into one style property. There are six primary shorthand CSS-style properties you might use:

- The **font** property defines the font style, variant, weight, size, line-height, and family (**http://about.com/webdesign/font**).

- The **margin** and **padding** properties define the space around the top, right, bottom, and left sides of an element (**http://about.com/webdesign/margin** and **http://about.com/webdesign/padding**).
- The **border** property defines the border around all four sides of an element and indicates the border width, style, and color (**http://about.com/webdesign/border**).
- The **list-style** property defines the position, list type, and image for list elements (**http://about.com/webdesign/liststyle**).
- The **background** property defines the background color, image, repeat, attachment, and position (**http://about.com/webdesign/background**).

Don't make lots of requests to the server. When you're writing HTML, every time you have an element that points to something else on the server like an image, video, or sound file, the Web browser must work with the server to get that element. Every query to the server takes time, whether it's sending the request, the server interpreting the request, or the browser displaying the results of the request. The more HTTP requests you have on a page, the more the browser has to wait.

Make sure your ads and external elements load fast. One of the biggest mistakes that a speed-conscious Web developer can make is to forget about the ads. Most ads are served by a different Web server than the one hosting your Web site. If that server slows down or fails, it can impact the speed of your entire site. One way to solve this problem is to load your ads in an inline frame. This way, the Web browser can display a box for the ad, and if the ad server has issues, the box remains empty.

ELSEWHERE ON THE WEB

▶ Those of you who are serious about speeding up your Web pages might want to look into HTTP compression (**www.webreference.com/internet/software/servers/http/compression/index.html**). Most Web browsers support HTTP compression. If you run an Apache server or your site is hosted on one, ask your administrator if mod_gzip (**http://sourceforge.net/projects/mod-gzip/index.html**) is installed on the server. This can be used to send compressed HTML.

Get Linked

Speedy Web pages will always be important. While our customers keep upgrading to faster and faster connections, we designers keep adding content that requires faster connections.

OPTIMIZE YOUR SITE

There are more tips and tricks you can do to speed up your Web pages, and the links on this page will keep you up to date.
http://about.com/webdesign/optforspeed

OPTIMIZING IMAGES FOR SPEED

The first place to look when speeding up your Web site is the images. If your images aren't fast, the rest of your site won't be either.
http://about.com/webdesign/imageopt

Chapter 13

Making Your Site Accessible

Why Build Accessible Web Pages?

Before I start a chapter on accessibility in Web design, it's important that you understand what I mean by accessibility and what I'll be discussing. I am an American and have some understanding of U.S. law, but I am not a lawyer. Laws change, and if you live in a country other than the United States or your Web site will be serving people outside the country (which, given that the Web is global, is more likely than you might think), the laws that govern you or your Web site may be different. This chapter isn't about laws. This chapter is about making sure that you're not setting up a Web site that shuts people out before they've even entered the door.

Accessibility is just what it sounds like: providing access to your Web site and making sure that people get the information you're trying to provide. Unfortunately, many Web designers when they think about accessibility think two things: "ugly, boring Web sites" and "for blind people."

The good news is that the pages that you've built in this book are written to be accessible. You may think they're ugly (that's your opinion); that's not because they are accessible but rather because you don't like my design aesthetic (which just indicates your poor taste). Seriously, though, it's very easy to use CSS to style accessible, beautiful Web pages. The act of separating the design elements (in the CSS) from the content elements (in the HTML) is a first step in making your pages accessible.

Another bonus you get from making your Web pages accessible is that search engines like accessible Web pages.

Accessible Doesn't Just Mean Blind

One of the first misconceptions about writing accessible Web pages is that it refers to writing for blind people using screen readers. In reality, writing an accessible Web page is important to many different kinds of people (and technology as well):

- **The visually impaired:** Those who are blind as well as those will less than 20/20 vision
- **The hearing impaired:** Those who have difficulty hearing sounds on Web sites
- **The movement impaired:** Those with tremors or difficulties holding or using a mouse
- **Non-English speakers:** Those who experience barriers when visiting sites intended for a single-language audience
- **Search engines and other robots:** Search engines send spiders to crawl Web sites, and if your site is inviting to them it could help you find more customers.

▶ Before you get worried that accessibility is going to be another one of those difficult things you have to do to maintain a Web site, check out my article "Accessible HTML" (http://about.com/webdesign/accessiblehtml). It is one of the first articles I ever wrote for the About .com Web Design/HTML site, but it's still valid. If you were only to follow those instructions, you'd be well on the way to an accessible Web site. It's not that hard!

Blind people read the Web, too. The Web pages are read to them using a screen reader. The best known screen reader is JAWS (**www.freedomscientific.com/fs_products/software_jaws.asp**), a Windows application that reads aloud information on the screen. Screen readers, while improving all the time, are not as good as a human brain for processing what they see on the screen. So a Web designer who is writing accessible Web pages needs to be aware that everything visual on the screen should have a text counterpoint. This includes images, Flash animations, and even icons and layout, all of which can have an affect on how the screen reader renders the page.

You may not realize that being blind does not always mean you can see nothing. I had a cousin who was legally blind but who could see distances well enough to get a driver's license. Another friend who is legally blind is a very good technical writer. She uses a magnifying lens to see what she's reading or writing. A Web designer who recognizes that there are varying degrees of vision impairment, and who builds Web pages to support that, is a much more accessible designer than one who designs "one size fits all" Web sites.

But what if you can't hear? Many Web sites don't have a lot of sound on them, and so this may not seem to be an issue. But before you skip this section, ask yourself whether your site includes any sound at all. Before you say no, consider these options:

- Do you have any video with sound or are you planning on including any?
- Do you use or plan to use Flash animations? (Most have some sound associated with them.)
- Are there any sounds used for accents?
- Do you have or plan to put up a podcast?

When I started building Web pages in 1995, sound was very difficult to use. Some pages had sound, but it was typically an annoying midi that you were more concerned with turning off than listening to. Today, podcasts and video are so easy to add and use that it's a lot easier to create a Web site that is inaccessible to the hearing impaired.

And what if you can't move a mouse? Frankly, I hate pages that require the use of a mouse, and I'm not movement impaired in any way. I don't like removing my hands from the keyboard. I am much faster when I can leave my hands in one place and do all my work from there. I also find that my wrists start to hurt when I use the mouse a lot, and since I don't want a repetitive stress injury, I avoid using the mouse.

Some people cannot use a mouse or find it very difficult. Making sure that your Web pages can be accessed with alternative devices such as the keyboard will help improve your site for motor-impaired people.

Language and cultures can be an access barrier, too. The global nature of the Web is a good thing. But if you're trying to make your site open to as many people as possible, you should be aware that people who don't speak the language of your site will still access it. I get e-mails from customers from all over the world. My mom's Cystic Fibrosis site has also received visitors from around the world, and her site is a lot smaller than mine.

About.com offers our Web sites only in English and doesn't provide translations, so my customers need some English to access my Web site. But I still need to be aware of other cultures and languages. When I build a new page, I keep in mind that some colors, word choices, or images might be offensive to other cultures.

ELSEWHERE ON THE WEB

▶ Auditory disabilities can be very hard to understand. The WebAIM Auditory Disabilities Web site (www.webaim.org/articles/auditory) is a great resource. It helps you understand when your Web page might be inaccessible to someone with hearing problems and also gives solutions for how to improve your site.

Writing Accessible Web Pages

Writing accessible Web pages doesn't require much beyond what we've already done for the pages we've built in this book. The main thing you need to do when writing accessible Web pages is think about how your page might appear to someone with accessibility issues. There are a few common mistakes that developers make when building Web pages. Consider the following:

- **Images require alternative text.** Beyond being required for valid XHTML, the alt attribute is the main way that images are accessible to screen readers and visually impaired people. Screen readers read the alternative text when it's there. Make sure that you always have alternative text that makes sense within the context of your Web document. It's easy to write alt text. Just make sure to always use the alt attribute on your image tags, like so: `<img src="image.gif" alt="Image" />` .
- **Image maps need alt text too.** Many Web designers forget to use alt text in image maps to make them accessible. But it's easy to add alt text to image maps : `<area shape="rect" coords="0,0,20,30" href= "http://webdesign.about .com/cs/imagemaps/a/aabg051899a.htm" alt= "Help Building Image Maps" />` .
- **Create a low-vision layout for your site.** Low-vision layouts are versions of your Web page that are redesigned to make them more accessible to people with poorer vision. These layouts are ideal because they provide an alternative that someone with low vision is free to choose or not, as desired.
- **Watch for color issues for colorblind people.** Remember that people who are colorblind may have issues with your page if you use colors to differentiate content. Watch the

use of reds and greens and be aware when color is the only thing that makes something stand out on your Web page.

- **Include noframes on your framed pages.** Frames can be very inaccessible. So if you use frames, make sure to include a noframes option for screen readers and search engines that can't read frames.
- **Image-heavy pages should have text-only alternative pages.** Put links to text versions of your Web pages near the top of the page so that screen readers can find them quickly.
- **Audio and video files should include a transcript or, even better, captioning.** Transcripts or captions make audio and video files accessible when otherwise they would be completely unusable.
- **Use the accesskey attribute to help access form fields and links.** The accesskey attribute (<u>http://about.com/webdesign/ accesskey</u>) makes links and form fields accessible through mouse clicks, similar to shortcut keys in computer programs.

Dealing with vision issues is the first step to accessibility. You may be surprised to realize that a lot of people viewing your Web site have some vision problem. Vision problems can range from blurry vision, migraines, low vision, or blind spots to actual blindness.

Web designers are often young, or at least not old enough to need reading glasses. But guess what? Even if you don't need glasses, chances are that at least half of your audience does. The largest-growing segment of the Internet is retired people, and most of them need some form of assistance in reading small print. I'm not yet old enough to require reading glasses, but the popularity of ant-sized fonts on the Web is amazing to me. I regularly use the Ctrl-+ key in Firefox to make fonts larger, and I have 20/20 vision.

First, make sure that the fonts can be resized. This does not mean that you need to make them huge; keep your font sizes the size that you like, even if that is ant-sized. Instead, make sure that your Web-site layout is flexible enough to handle larger font sizes. The easiest way to do this is to build your page, and then view it in Firefox. Once there, click Ctrl-+ once or twice to see what happens when the font gets bigger. (If you're using a fixed-width layout, the text will eventually go over or under the images that are beside the text. This is a drawback to fixed-width layouts.)

Once you've designed text that is large enough for you, but also resizable, look at your images. First check that all your images have alt text that fits in the context of the page and that also provides information about the image. Turn the images off, and view your Web page that way. Follow these steps to turn off images in Firefox:

1. Open the Tools menu.
2. Click on Options . . .
3. Change to the Content tab.
4. Uncheck the box called "Load Images."
5. Click OK and reload your Web page.

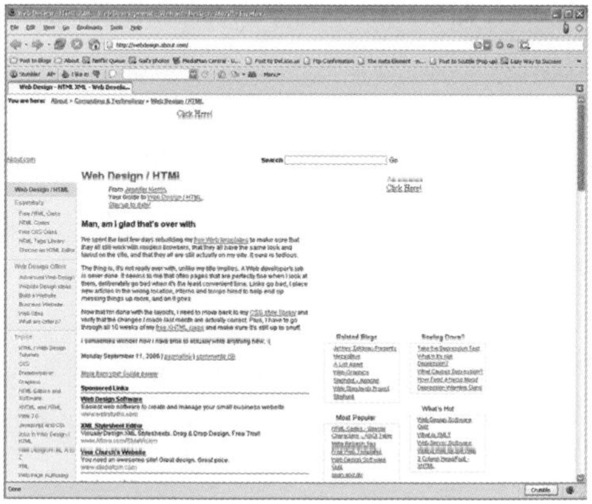

Figure 13-1: My home page without images: Not good, but it still works

If the page still works, then you have enough information in your alt text. If you don't, you should rethink the images.

As you can see, the About.com Web Design/HTML home page still works with the images turned off. Many of the images do not have alt text because the design and HTML of the page is controlled by the About.com design team, not me. But since most of these images are ads, icons, or backgrounds, they don't need alt text. The only thing I wish had alt text is my photo, but since my name is printed out right next to it, that isn't all that bad either.

Once you've fixed your images, look at the color choices on your page. Color blindness affects between 8 and 12 percent of males of European descent. But it's very common to see an error message that reads something like "Please fill in the form fields marked in red below." Depending upon the type of colorblindness, the red text you have on your page may look nearly identical to the surrounding black text. The easiest way to solve this is to always use another cue along with color to make your points stand out. This could be as simple as adding bold or an icon along with the red color.

One other area of vision issues that many Web-site designers seem to forget is migraines. I get visual migraines that turn my vision from normal 20/20 to a complete blur of colors in a line across my sight. If I'm very lucky (and take medicine quickly) this doesn't turn into a debilitating headache. The challenge is that flickering lights can trigger a migraine, and this includes flickering images on Web pages. I've been to Web pages where the bright colors and flickering animated gifs were so bad that I did get the beginnings of a migraine. Every time, I left immediately. You may love to build and look at bright, flickering Web pages, but if 18 percent of women and 6 to 8 percent of men will leave your site immediately because of them, is it worth it?

Make sure your site is accessible to people with auditory problems. Like our vision, our hearing gets worse as we grow older. This is something that we need to be aware of as we add more multimedia to our sites. Things like video, podcasts, and audio files can be completely useless to someone with hearing impairment. And captioning is an easy way to solve that problem.

With captions, you put a real-time text version of what is being said onto the video or flash animation. There are many tools available to help you do it, the most popular of which is MAGpie (http:// ncam.wgbh.org/webaccess/magpie). MAGpie allows Web authors to caption video saved as QuickTime, Windows Media Player, or RealPlayer.

Make sure your pages are accessible to people with motor difficulties. This can run the range from someone who has tremors and can't control a mouse with fine motor control all the way through someone who may only access the computer through a mouth stylus or voice because of paralysis or other problem. Web pages can be extremely challenging when they have things like image maps that require people to click in a very small area or when forms and links do not have access keys set to make them easy to get to and start typing.

Here are some easy solutions to making your pages more usable for motor-impaired people:

- Use the tabindex attribute (http://about.com/webdesign/tabindex). This attribute defines the order that links should be tabbed to on a Web page. This allows you to skip navigation with one keystroke.
- Avoid image maps. The small areas can be hard to click on, and it can be hard to even tell they are links.

- If you must use image maps, make the link areas big. Also, always include a default area that leads to a text navigation page. If users click on the wrong spot, they can get to the right one easily. `<area shape="default" href="http://webdesign.about.com/od/htmltags/p/bltags_area.htm" alt="More about the area tag" />`
- Link your images. Rather than an image map, make your images one link to one place. They are easier to see and usually bigger and so easier to click on.

Global Web Pages

When you are writing a Web page that will go on the World Wide Web, you are, by definition, writing for a global audience. This applies even if you never have any intention of translating your pages and your company doesn't have any interest in selling outside of your current area.

There are a number of things to be aware of when building your Web site to be accessible and usable to the widest possible audience.

What is your topic? Culture can play a large part in whether or not your Web site will be a hit in a country other than your own. This even applies to regions of the same country. To use a non-Web example, I heard a radio story about a community where neighbors regularly met in the middle of the street at night to chat and talk. Unfortunately, the police officers were from a different area of the county where that was seen as gang activity. If your Web site is about meeting with your neighbors, you definitely don't want the police shutting it down due to suspected criminal intentions.

This means that if your topic is something that might be regionally specific, make that clear. This is especially true if you're dealing with something that is illegal in one country but not in another. For example, when a friend of mine was planning to go to Singapore a few years ago, he found out that they required men to cut their hair to above the neckline. Since his hair was much longer than that, he changed his plans. Because they posted their laws, he was able to make that decision without any negative repercussions to himself.

Language is an obvious barrier. Your site might be viewed by someone in another country who does not speak English (or the language of your Web site). Even trickier is that even if you're writing in English, your site may be viewed by English speakers all over the world. Writing in slang is a great way to make your site completely incomprehensible, even to a native English speaker. If they aren't familiar with the slang terms you are using, it doesn't matter that they are from Canada or Australia or Singapore. Slang can also be very difficult for non-native English speakers to understand.

If you decide that you want to translate your Web site, you'll run into even more issues. First, always use a professional translator rather than an automated translation program. The automated systems work fine for short text blocks, but they usually end up with very strange text that has been literally translated word for word.

Watch for generic terms. A lot of seemingly generic terms won't make sense to a global audience:

- **Regional designations:** "East Coast" means New York to me and Queensland to an Australian.
- **Specifying something as "foreign" or "domestic":** I was the foreigner when I lived in Uzbekistan, and my friend Muhayo was the native.

▸ Writing Web pages for an international audience takes some thought, and there are a couple of other pages on my site that can help. If you want to write in non-English languages, you'll need to know how to add special characters to your Web pages (http://about.com/webdesign/characters) as well as what codes to use (http://about.com/webdesign/characterhtml).

- **Place names:** Moscow could mean Russia or Idaho, and there is a Portland in nearly every state in the United States.

Date codes are different around the world. If I write the date as 12-09-1971, do I mean September 12 or December 9? This depends upon where you are in the world. The best way to write dates is to use the name of the month.

Address forms can be challenging for international users. One common sight you might see on a Web order form is an address section. Many forms have a drop-down menu listing the states, and some also include Canadian provinces. But if your Web site is global, some countries don't have a state or province designation. When I lived in Tashkent, Uzbekistan, my address had no state; it was "Tashkent, Uzbekistan." If you make the state field optional, that guarantees that someone from Moscow, Idaho, will forget to include her state in the order, and you won't know if it's Moscow, Russia, or Idaho, or someplace else named Moscow.

Some forms require a zip code, but if you accept orders from Canada, where they have postal codes, you're going to have a problem. And if you validate your form to require only numbers, Canadians will have more trouble, as their postal codes have letters in them. If you're opening your order forms up to even more countries, your forms need to be even less specific.

The best solution is to create multiple forms for the countries you ship to. That way you can have the most common country as the default form, and the others as options at the top of the form. For example, Amazon.com has a completely different site for its customers in the United Kingdom. The site is still in English, but you're not asked for your state or zip code when you make your order, and there isn't a list of U.S. states to be seen.

Validating Accessibility

How do you really know if your Web site is accessible? You can view your site with images or sound off; or, if your budget allows it, buy a screen reader to test your pages. But that is out of the range that most small businesses can afford to spend on making their sites accessible. It's an expense you'll have to bear, however, if your site falls into a class of sites required by law to meet accessibility guidelines. In the United States, that usually means government and government-funded Web sites.

It's important to understand Section 508 and what it means. Section 508 (www.section508.gov) is a U.S. law that requires all federal agencies to make electronic information available and accessible to people with disabilities. If your Web site is for a federal agency or affiliated with one, it must be Section-508 compliant. The best way to ensure that is to use an accessibility validator, such as WebXACT (http://webxact.watchfire.com).

Understand the W3C Web content accessibility guidelines (WCAG). If you understand WCAG (www.w3.org/TR/WAI-WEBCONTENT), you'll be one step closer to accessible content. Because creating accessible Web content goes beyond writing the correct HTML tags, you need to think about how your Web pages will be accessed and make allowances for people who might be using different methods. I've created a list of WCAG guidelines to help you check and see if your site is accessible.

- **Provide equivalent alternatives to auditory and visual content.** This is the most basic requirement. Any content that is not actual text on your Web page should be explained with alternative text or captions.

- **Don't rely on color alone.** Make sure that any color codes you have on your text or images are for decoration. If they are there to indicate something else, make sure there is another distinction, such as an icon, bolded text, or underlining, to make it stand out.
- **Use markup and style sheets and do so properly.** Avoid using deprecated HTML tags and styles. If you've followed the instructions in this book, you'll be using CSS and HTML properly.
- **Clarify natural language usage.** Always be sure to define what language the page is written in using the lang attribute on your HTML tag. For example, `<html lang="en">` would represent English.
- **Create tables that transform gracefully.** Tables can be difficult to make accessible. But it is possible. Use all the table tags available to you (**http://about.com/webdesign/tabletag**) such as caption, tbody, thead, and tfoot, to differentiate the different sections of your table. Only use tables for data, not for page layout.
- **Ensure that pages featuring new technologies transform gracefully.** Some technologies, like Flash and Ajax, may not be new to you, but they aren't reliably supported in many assistive devices. My rule of thumb is that unless I've tested it in a screen reader or other assistive device, I always have an alternative for any technology I have on my site beyond plain HTML and CSS.
- **Ensure user control of time-sensitive content changes.** If your Web page is going to change after a specific amount of time, make sure that this can be stopped or slowed down by your readers. For example, a page that automatically refreshes after two minutes might be plenty of time for you

to read the content, but it might cut someone else off after only a few sentences.

- **Ensure direct accessibility of embedded user interfaces.** If you use any other applications inside your Web pages like PDF, video, or Flash, these should also follow all accessibility guidelines.
- **Design for device-independence.** No matter what type of device your customer is using to view your Web page, it should still be usable. For example, have you tried going to your Web site in your Web-ready phone or mobile device? That can be a scary experience.
- **Use interim solutions. Keep aware of the issues that browsers and screen readers have.** For example, some screen readers won't allow readers to navigate to empty text boxes, while others won't block pop-up windows automatically. There are some interim solutions: Do not use pop-up windows; write form labels immediately before the form element; provide linear text alternatives to tables; use default (accesskey) characters for editable text areas; and place non-linked text characters between adjacent links.
- **Use W3C technologies and guidelines.** Don't use HTML tags (like marquee) that are not part of the W3C standard. And don't use items that have not been made into a recommendation by the W3C. For example, as of this writing, CSS 3 is not yet a recommendation, but some Web browsers support some parts of it. To be accessible, don't use CSS 3 properties until it is a recognized standard.
- **Provide context and orientation information.** Title your pages, frames, and tables. If it's appropriate, use relationship tags in the head of your pages to define which page comes before the current one and which comes after, and so on.

- **Provide clear navigation mechanisms.** Make sure your navigation is consistent from page to page. It should be clear outside of the context of the rest of the content where other links on the page lead.
- **Ensure that documents are clear and simple.** Always strive for clarity in your Web pages. The Web is hard to read for nearly everyone, at least harder to read than a paperback book, and the simpler your pages are, the faster your customers will get the information they want. And that's good for everyone.

Accessibility does not have to be hard, and it doesn't mean that your site will be ugly. But making your site accessible makes it easier for everyone to view it, and happy readers means more readers.

Get Linked

Accessibility is about making your Web pages available in a way that most people can use. The following links will provide more information and help getting your pages accessible.

ACCESSIBILITY LINKS

New articles and information about accessibility and usability are coming out all the time. These links will help you keep informed about accessibility and how to keep your site accessible.

http://about.com/webdesign/accessusability

LOCALIZING WEB SITES

Creating a Web site for an international audience is an access issue, even if it's not legally accessibility. These links will help you create pages for audiences beyond English speakers.

http://about.com/webdesign/localization

ACCESSIBILITY VALIDATORS

WebXACT is a great validator, but there are others out there. There is even one that will show you how your page will look to someone who is color blind.

http://about.com/webdesign/accessvalidators

Chapter 14

Adding Drama: Flash, DHTML, Ajax, and More

What Are DHTML, Flash, and Ajax?

Some people would argue that these technologies are the most interesting part of Web development. These programs run the behavior layer of Web sites.

I've discussed the structure layer (the HTML and content of your pages) and the style layer (CSS and how your pages look), but up until now we've only dealt with behavior layer in terms of some JavaScript.

JavaScript and other client-side scripting languages are the easiest way to create Web-page behaviors because they don't require any interaction with the Web server. JavaScript is called a client-side scripting language because all of the functionality happens within the Web browser or client. This means you don't need Web-server support to create behaviors on your Web site. But

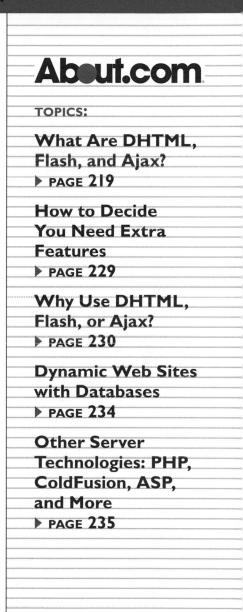

if your customers' Web browsers don't support the scripting language you're using, they won't see any of the behaviors.

What about DHTML? Dynamic HTML (DHTML) is a method of using JavaScript to work with the **document object model (DOM)** to create behaviors on Web sites.

DHTML menus are one way to do this, and it's possible to create roll-over menus without any JavaScript at all. The HTML for our navigation is a great place to start to create menus that have additional drop-down options.

```
<ul id="navigation">
<li><a href="/index.html">Home</a></li>
<li><a href="/products/index.html">Dog Toys for
Sale</a></li>
<li><a href="/articles/index.html">Dog Informa-
tion</a></li>
<li><a href="/about/index.html">About This
Site</a></li>
</ul>
```

This navigation menu has only the top level elements in it. But each lower level of the navigation is just another unordered list inside it. Here's what my final navigation looks like:

```
<ul id="navigation">
<li><a href="/index.html">Home</a></li>
<li><a href="/products/index.html">Dog Toys for
Sale &gt;&gt;</a>
  <ul>
  <li><a href="/products/stuffed.html">Stuffed
Toys</a></li>
  <li><a href="/products/balls.html">Balls</a></
li>
  <li><a href="/products/tugs.html">Tug Toys</
a></li>
  <li><a href="/products/entertain.html">Boredom
Reducers</a></li>
```

```
  </ul>
</li>
<li><a href="/articles/index.html">Dog Informa-
tion &gt;&gt;</a>
  <ul>
  <li><a href="/articles/health.html">Health</
a></li>
  <li><a href="/articles/breeds/index.
html">Breeds &gt;&gt;</a>
    <ul>
    <li><a href="/articles/breeds/bordercollie.
html">Border Collie</a></li>
    <li><a href="/articles/breeds/labrador.
html">Labrador</a></li>
    </ul>
  </li>
  <li><a href="/articles/training.
html">Training</a></li>
  </ul>
</li>
<li><a href="/about/index.html">About This Site
&gt;&gt;</a>
  <ul>
  <li><a href="/about/copyright.
html">Copyright</a></li>
  <li><a href="/about/privacy.html">Privacy
Policy</a></li>
  <li><a href="/about/contact.html">Contact Us</
a></li>
  </ul>
</li>
</ul>
```

As you can see, only the "Home" link doesn't have a second
level, and the "Breeds" link has a third level. If you apply the style
sheet we used in Chapter 8 to the above HTML, you'll end up with
a strange hybrid of lists and sub-lists. But by altering the CSS a bit,
you can create a drop-down navigation list.

```
ul#navigation, ul#navigation ul {
  width: 175px;
```

▶ Creating CSS menus is easy. The method described here works great for IE 7, Mozilla 1, Opera 7, and Safari 1. Only IE 6 and 5 don't handle the :hover pseudo-class correctly. If you want to learn more about how to create DHTML menus using CSS, check out my article "Standards Based DHTML Menus" (http://about.com/webdesign/dhtmlmenus). You can also see the above example online (Example 14-1, http://about.com/webdesign/example14-1code) and with a horizontal menu in Example 14-2 (http://about.com/web design/example14-2code).

```css
  background: #fff url(navbg.gif);
  padding-left: 0px;
  margin-left: 0px;
  border-left: 1px solid black;
}
ul#navigation li {
  list-style-type: none;
  margin: 0px;
  padding-left: 5px;
  position: relative;
  color: #63c;
  font-weight: bold;
  height: 20px;
}
ul#navigation li ul { display: none; } /* hide
from IE 6/5 */
ul#navigation li > ul {
  display: none;
  position: absolute;
  top: 2px;
  left: 170px;
}
ul#navigation li > ul li { height: 20px; }
ul#navigation li:hover{ background: #fff
url(navbg_over.gif); color: #000; }
ul#navigation li:hover > ul { display: block; }
ul#navigation li a {
  color: #63c;
  display: block;
  width: 100%;
  text-decoration: none;
}
ul#navigation li a:hover { color: #000; }
ul#navigation li:hover > a { color: #000; }
```

Another simple JavaScript writes the date to your Web page. It's only one line:

```html
<script type="text/javascript">document.
write(new Date());</script>
```

This will display the current day, date, time (down to the seconds), and time zone. Instead, we can use JavaScript to write out the current date in a friendlier format, like "December 16, 2007."

```
<script type="text/javascript">
var date = new Date();
var month = new Array(7);
month[0] = "January";
month[1] = "February";
month[2] = "March";
month[3] = "April";
month[4] = "May";
month[5] = "June";
month[6] = "July";
month[7] = "August";
month[8] = "September";
month[9] = "October";
month[10] = "November";
month[11] = "December";
var year = date.getYear();
if (year < 2000) { year+-1900; }
document.write(month[date.getMonth()] + " " +
date.getDate() + ", " + year);
</script>
```

One way to use a date script on your Web page is shown online in Example 14-3 (http://about.com/webdesign/example14-3 code).

A great way to interact with your Web page directly using JavaScript and the DOM is to use JavaScript to improve your Web forms. Two behaviors that help Web forms are putting the cursor in the first field and then validating the fields as they are filled out.

Putting the cursor in the first field is easy. You need to give your form an id so that you can reference it in your JavaScript.

```
<form action="mailto:webdesign.guide@about.com"
method="get" enctype="text/plain" id="contactus"
name="contactus">
```

On our "Contact Us" form, the first form field is the "name" field, and it has the ID "name." To focus on that line, you add a line to your body tag telling the browser to look for the "name" form field when the page has loaded and put the cursor there.

```
<body onload="document.contactus.name.focus();">
```

As you can see online in Example 14-4 (<u>http://about.com/web design/example14-4code</u>), this makes it much easier for your customers to start filling in the Web form. Instead of first clicking in the field, they can just start typing.

For my final JavaScript example, I'll show you how to make a very simple validator that checks as your readers use the form to see that the required fields are filled. If the required content isn't there, an error message automatically appears on the page.

First you need to build your form and add an onblur attribute to each field that is required.

```
<form action="mailto:webdesign.guide@about.com"
method="get" enctype="text/plain" id="contactus"
name="contactus">
<label accesskey="f" for="first name">First
Name:
<input type="text" name="first name" id="first
name" value="" size="40" onblur="validateForm(th
is); " /></label><br />
<label accesskey="l" for="last name">Last Name:
<input type="text" name="last name" id="last
name" value="" size="40" onblur="validateForm(th
is); " /></label><br />
<label accesskey="e" for="email">Email:
<input type="text" name="email" id="email"
value="" size="40" onblur="validateForm(this); "
/></label><br />
```

```
Do you want a reply?
<label accesskey="y"><input type="radio"
name="reply" id="reply" value="yes" /> Yes</
label>
<label accesskey="n"><input type="radio"
name="reply" id="reply" value="no"
checked="checked" /> No</label><br />
What is your message?<br />
<textarea name="message" id="message" rows="10"
cols="35" onblur="validateForm(this);"></
textarea><br />
<input type="submit" value="Send Message" />
<input type="reset" value="Clear Form" />
</form>
```

Every field in my form is required, so all of them have the code `onblur="validateForm(this);    "` in them. The only exception is the radio button. I added a `checked="checked"` attribute to the "no" option. If they want a reply, they have to change it to "yes." The onblur attribute tells the browser to run a JavaScript function when the focus is removed from that element.

The script will then display an error message to the right of the form fields indicating that the field is required. But in order to do this, we need to provide an area for the script to add content. I did this by adding an empty <div> container above my <form> tag:

```
<div id="check"></div>
```

I then styled it to float to the right and have a width of 250 pixels. Since it's empty in the default HTML, nothing will display. But when the validateForm function runs, if the field is empty, an error message will display in that div.

The validateForm function looks like this:

```
function validateForm(checkMe) {
  // check that the field is filled in
```

```
  var checkElement = document.
getElementById("check");
  var br = document.createElement("br");
  if (checkMe.value == "") {
    // it's empty so display an error message
    var gotitText = document.
createTextNode("Please fill in the " + checkMe.
name + " field. ");
    checkElement.appendChild(gotitText);
    checkElement.appendChild(br);
  }
}
```

It is saved in a script file that is attached in the head of my Web page with a <script> tag:

```
<script type="text/javascript" src="zexample14-
5.js"> </script>
```

You can see the form online in Example 14-5 (http://about.com/webdesign/example14-5code). This page includes the entire JavaScript file, the XHTML, and the CSS I used to style the page.

Flash is harder to add, but it can do a lot more. Flash is a very complex program that can create animations, applications, and forms for your Web site. Unlike JavaScript, Flash is not text based, so I can't type examples into this book. Flash is a great tool for adding audio and video to your site. Because it is interactive, you can use it for forms or applications that you can't do with plain HTML and JavaScript.

You must learn Flash to build Flash applications for your Web site. Start by downloading a free trial version from the Adobe Web site (www.adobe.com). It is possible to create SWF files (the Flash file type) with other programs, called Flash authoring tools, but I don't recommend it. Flash offers you a lot of flexibility and functionality. Plus, if you have the most recent version of Flash, you'll have the most recent features in Flash applications available to you. Third-party applications won't always have these right away.

When adding Flash to your Web site, consider doing it gradually. Add it where it will add value, not because you think it is fun to build. Here are some applications that are well suited to Flash:

- Video in Flash is easy on your customers. Now that Flash is so common, putting your video in Flash makes a lot more sense.
- Animation in Flash is prettier than GIF animation. Because Flash uses vector graphics, the quality of the images is better, and longer animated sequences will be smaller as a flash application than an animated GIF.
- Stand-alone applications work better as Flash than other programming. This is especially true of games.

Ajax brings us back to JavaScript but with a twist. Ajax combines JavaScript with server-side programming to create Web pages that are more like applications than the traditional static Web pages we're used to.

In a traditional Web application, the customer reads the page and interacts with a form or other element. Eventually she clicks on something. The browser then sends that click and the other entered information to the server. The server reviews the information, processes it, and sends back a new page to the browser. The browser then displays the new Web page to the customer. And the process starts all over again.

In an Ajax application, there is still interaction between the browser and the Web server, but it happens behind the scenes. When your customer comes to the Web page, she begins interacting with it. As soon as data is entered into the form, the Java Script script starts sending data to the Web server. It does this

WHAT'S HOT

▶ The exception to my rule about using Flash to create Flash applications concerns external Flash tools. These are tools that add extra features to Flash or make the existing features easier to use. For example, it's easy to create a screensaver in Flash using some of the screensaver tools listed on my Flash tools page (http://about.com/webdesign/flashtoolsindex).

through an asynchronous request using the `XMLHttpRequest` or other method to request data from the Web server. The Web server then works in the background to process the request and sends it back to the Web browser. All this time, the customer is still filling out the form or otherwise interacting with the Web page. When the data arrives, the page is updated without reloading it, so there is no disconnect for the customer.

You may be wondering how this is different from JavaScript. Remember how JavaScript typically works on Web pages. JavaScript can only save data in a temporary memory location on the local machine viewing the Web page. As soon as your customer goes to another page or turns off the browser, the data that JavaScript had is gone. Many Web developers got around this by using Web cookies to store data, but cookies got a bad reputation for invading privacy, so they aren't used as much. The other problem with cookies is that they don't store the data in a fashion that's usable to the Web developer after the customer has left the Web site. The only way to do that is to have the Web page interact with the server using a server-side program like PHP, Perl, or JSP.

Ajax uses the server-side programs as well, but instead of having the Web server send back entire Web pages, it sends data in the form of XML. The JavaScript on the Web page accepts that data and uses it to interact with the DOM to change bits of the Web page. So instead of having to wait for an entire page to load, the customer gets nearly instant feedback.

How to Decide You Need Extra Features

All these advanced features can be a lot of fun both to contemplate and to build. But you always need to think about whether you need them or not. Having a Web site that is very Flash intensive or fully Ajax enabled might make you feel like a powerful developer, but if you have no content to back it up, no one will visit your site.

Another problem that happens when a developer gets overly excited about new features is that the site becomes a features playground with no point. In my article "When to Use Ajax and When Not To" (http://about.com/webdesign/useajax), I mention an Ajax script I wrote. The script updated a Web page to indicate there was new mail in a certain e-mail account. At the same time, I kept that e-mail account open in the background on my desktop. When a new message came in, I would answer it and delete it immediately. The chance that new mail would be there when someone started using the Web page was so low that the feature was useless.

Unless you are building a Web site solely for yourself, always consider what your customers are looking for. It's safe to say that they are not looking for technology for technology's sake. Your dramatic elements should serve a purpose. When I'm tempted to build a Web site with a lot of technology, first I see if I can do it any other way. Remember the hierarchy of technology we discussed in Chapter 4?

1. HTML
2. CSS
3. Client-side scripts
4. Web applications
5. Server-side scripts

The technology we're discussing here is level three (JavaScript and some Flash), four (Ajax and some Flash), or five (Ajax and CGI scripts). If you can solve your problems with level one or two technologies, then your site will load faster and be easier to maintain.

I have found that it's easiest to think about the new technologies if I first think about how I would handle the problem without them. For example, when building a form that is going to send an e-mail, the first level of technology would be to have no validation on the form because HTML and CSS cannot validate form data alone. Since this makes the form less useful, I would then use JavaScript to validate the form data. If I needed more interaction while the form was being filled out, I might convert the form to Flash or Ajax, but only after I'd determined that I couldn't do it with HTML, CSS, or JavaScript.

Why Use DHTML, Flash, or Ajax?

There are so many technologies out there that it can be hard to decide which one to use. If you're going to be building them yourself, it can be hard to decide where to start. There is so much to learn. If you're going to use DHTML, Flash, or Ajax on your Web site you should know what each is best at so that you can choose the right one for the job.

Use DHTML for situations in the browser window. DHTML is the least complex of all the technology options discussed here. But that doesn't mean it's easy. What makes DHTML less complex is that you only need to worry about what is happening inside the Web browser and what Web browser your customer is using at the time. You don't need any special server applications or programs to write DHTML; you just need to know XHTML, JavaScript, and the DOM.

DHTML doesn't require any interaction with the Web server. When you're considering adding DHTML, you need to make sure that what you need doesn't require any server interaction. Here are some common uses for DHTML:

- **Modifying the style of the Web page:** You might provide your customers with a button to resize the text or change the color of your site to make it more readable.

ELSEWHERE ON THE WEB

▶ When you start building a site with advanced technology, build it in a form called progressive enhancement (www.adobe.com/devnet/flash/articles/progressive_enhancement.html). When you use progressive enhancement, you build a site that uses HTML and CSS as the baseline, and then add JavaScript, Flash, Ajax, or other technology to it in small doses. You want to make sure that you're always designing for the HTML and CSS layers. The rest adds value to the site.

- **Building navigation systems:** It is now common to see menus using just CSS and some JavaScript.
- **Creating animation:** All you need is one or two images to create a basic animation.
- **Validating forms on the fly:** The preceding example illustrates how DHTML can be used for this purpose.

Don't use DHTML if your customers aren't on modern browsers (Such as Internet Explorer 6 and up and Mozilla or Safari 1 and up). Before those Web browsers were commonly available, DHTML was very difficult to write because there were very few standards. If your Web site is catering to an older browser demographic, then you should avoid DHTML or do a lot of testing on your browser targets before you release any pages. Even if you are targeting newer browsers, always test your pages in older browsers. Those customers should see *something,* even if it's not the slick DHTML interface you created.

Flash is best for high-quality animations. Flash uses vector-based graphics, which scale better than bitmap graphics (GIF, JPEG, and PNG) without looking blocky or choppy. When you animate a vector graphic in Flash, you have more control over how it looks because you can control the number of frames it should take to move from one shape to another.

Another big benefit of using Flash on your Web site is that you get a lot more control over the precise size and shape of your graphics and fonts. It is possible to embed fonts into Flash documents so that they look exactly as you created them no matter where they are viewed. Web pages don't have that ability. If the machine viewing your page doesn't have the font you specify, your text will show up in a different font. This is especially important if your company is branded by the font you use.

Some of the most popular uses of Flash on Web sites include these:

- Animated cartoons are popular on the Web in Flash. I read the StrongBad e-mails all the time (**www.homestarrunner .com/main2.html**), and that entire site is in Flash.
- Splash pages can introduce your Web site in Flash. But as discussed in Chapter 9, be careful that you don't alienate your customers with them.
- Audio and video files are easy to introduce using Flash. While it's possible to use the object tag to put audio and video on your site, using Flash gives you a lot more control.
- Many Web games are built in Flash.

I don't recommend using Flash for everything. If you don't have underlying HTML with text, your Flash Web pages can be difficult or impossible for search engines to spider. Using Flash for navigation can cause a lot of accessibility problems. Another issue with Flash applications is the missing "Back" button (**http://about .com/webdesign/backbutton**). People use that button in their Web browser all the time, but Flash doesn't support it. So when you click back in a Flash page, you are taken back to the previous Web page, even if the Flash application had several pages of content in it. And finally, internationalization can be challenging with Flash.

Have you gotten the "Ajax call?" This is where your boss calls you and says, "We need some of that new tech, Ajax, on our Web site. When are you going to build something?" If you're building a site with your customers as the focus, you won't hang up the phone and start writing code. Instead, think about all the issues discussed so far. Do you have a situation that calls for Ajax? Is Ajax the right solution to the problem? Can you solve the problem in some simpler fashion?

Ajax is good for a lot of things. With Ajax, focus on the behaviors or actions that need to happen. If you're going to use Ajax to display content, consider some other technology (like DHTML). Use Ajax for actions. Ajax is specifically for actions on your site that involve both the Web browser (using DHTML) and the Web server (using a server-side programming language like PHP or JSP). Some good uses of Ajax are the following:

- **Update contact information in a database.** You can be validating the fields as they are filled in, and if there are database field requirements, you can validate against those before the data is sent to the database.
- **Help with pages that are updating all the time**, like Web e-mail clients and events calendars. As the customer is reading what's currently in the inbox, the Ajax scripts are looking for new entries and adding them to the list.
- **Create news tickers** with Ajax connected to RSS feeds.

As I mentioned above, don't use Ajax for hiding or displaying content. The problem with doing this has to do with search engines and accessibility. If the content isn't on the Web page (whether in a hidden layer or visible), search engines and screen readers won't be able to see it. If the search engine can't see it, then it won't rank your page based on it. Also, it's very easy to write completely inaccessible Ajax. This is both because screen readers don't handle JavaScript and because it's easy to forget options like noscript and alternative text if you don't need it in your Web browser. When you're building an Ajax application, be sure to test it in as many different browsers, operating systems, and computers as you can so that you know that your application degrades gracefully.

WHAT'S HOT

▶ I was involved in a project in which we used Flash to display two words on a Web page. Depending upon how you got to the Web page, you got that section in one of twenty-one different languages. When we first built the Flash element, it was two words and something like two megabytes in size. Yes, megabytes. It took us a while to realize the problem was the number of character sets we needed for all the different languages. We were able to optimize it down to a smaller size (http://about .com/webdesign/flashfontopt) but it was difficult to get the same functionality.

Dynamic Web Sites with Databases

If DHTML, Flash, and Ajax weren't enough, you can also improve your Web sites by putting a database on the back end. Databases are storehouses of information, and Web pages are designed to display information, so they tend to be a good match.

There are a few good ways to tell if your site could use a database. Database-driven Web sites have a few things in common:

- They have a lot of data or content. This can be anything from products to articles to images.
- The content is very similar. Products all have the same type of information, as do articles and photo galleries.
- The content can be chunked into individual segments. Each product, article, or photograph is unique.

The first one is the biggie. If you don't have a lot of content, setting up a database can be a huge drain on your resources for very little benefit. Database-driven Web sites work best when there is so much content that it is difficult to maintain without a database. For me that might be 100 product pages; for you, that might be 1000 images.

But what if your host doesn't provide a database? While databases like mySQL are becoming much more prevalent on Web-hosting services, not all hosts provide database access to their customers. Even if your host doesn't provide database access, it is possible to set up a quasi-data-driven Web site without one. You do it with text files.

I have run several Web sites where the database lived on my local hard drive, and whenever I updated it, I would run a command to export the database out as a text file to load onto the Web server. Once on the Web server, the text file was accessed through either a CGI or a PHP script to read the data files and display the data on the appropriate Web pages.

Other Server Technologies: PHP, ColdFusion, ASP, and More

There are lots of other technologies that you can use on your Web site, many more than could be covered in one book on Web design. Some are more common on Web-hosting providers than others. If you decide you will want a server technology sometime in the future, make sure your hosting provider can support it.

PHP is one of the most common languages on the Web. One huge benefit to using PHP is that it is so common. There are thousands of ready-made scripts available for you to use, and there are tutorials all over the Web. PHP connects very easily with mySQL databases and makes writing dynamic Web pages a breeze.

PHP is a programming or scripting language that works within the HTML that we're used to writing. I find this makes it easy to pick up and understand, as you can write an HTML page and then put a PHP call in the middle, and as you get more and more confident replace more and more of the HTML with PHP.

ColdFusion connects very easily with Dream-weaver. When Macromedia (the original maker of Dreamweaver) bought Allaire (the original maker of ColdFusion), one of the first things they did was integrate the two programs. This means that while it's easy to make PHP or JSP or ASP Web pages with Dreamweaver, it's ridiculously easy to make ColdFusion pages. This is nice if you're a Dreamweaver developer as it means you don't need a separate authoring tool to create your CFM Web pages.

ELSEWHERE ON THE WEB

▶ Learning how to build a database-driven Web site is well beyond the scope of this book, but luckily there are a lot of sites where you can start, and in Appendix C, you'll find several books on the subject as well. If you want to start learning about databases, check out the article by the About.com Guide to Databases, titled "What Is a Database?" (http://about .com/databases/whatisadata base). And the About.com Guide to PHP/mySQL has a tutorial (http://about.com/ php/phpmysql) that will help you connect the database to your Web site.

ColdFusion is a server-side programming language that interacts with both the Web pages and the server to help you create applications out of your Web pages. It is not nearly as popular as PHP, so there aren't as many ready-made scripts or tutorials for it, but it does offer a lot of power and flexibility for your Web site. If you're considering ColdFusion, read my article "Beyond CGI to ColdFusion" (**http://about.com/webdesign/coldfusion**).

ASP is Microsoft's answer to server-technology. It is very popular on Microsoft Web servers. If your hosting provider runs on a Windows or IIS Web server, chances are ASP is on there as well. ASP stands for active server pages, and like PHP and Cold-Fusion it uses server-side scripts to create dynamic and interactive Web pages. A good place to start learning about ASP Web pages is on my site in the ASP category (**http://about.com/web design/aspindex**).

But we're not done yet. There are so many other programming languages used on Web pages it would be impossible to name them all. Here are some that are starting to gain popularity:

- JSP, or Java server pages, are server-side scripts based on Java (**http://about.com/java/j2eeprogramming**).
- Ruby is an up-and-coming programming language that many people are starting to use on Web sites (**http://about.com/ruby/whatisruby**), especially with the Web framework Rails.
- Python is an interpreted, object-oriented programming language. Many people are switching to Python for their server-side scripts (**http://about.com/python/pythonforbeginners**).
- Delphi is an object-oriented programming environment set up to build applications in the Microsoft .NET framework (**http://about.com/delphi/aboutdelphi**).

No matter what type of scripting environment you decide to use on your Web site, or even if you decide against using one, you'll have a lot of fun learning about it and how to improve your Web site. If you don't want to learn another language, but you do want to use a database or scripting language on your site, don't despair. Chapter 15 will help you find someone to help you continue to build your site.

Get Linked

There are so many ways you can improve your Web site and add interactivity. The following links are a starting place for learning more about what we touched on in the chapter.

PROGRAMMING ON THE WEB

There are lots of different languages you can learn to program on the Web. I have resources on many of them on my site.

http://about.com/webdesign/programming

AJAX

Ajax is, in many ways, a vindication of JavaScript. The articles and resources you'll find here will help you understand how to use Ajax and how JavaScript works with it.

http://about.com/webdesign/ajaxindex

Chapter 15

When to Hire Help

Assess Your Skills and Weaknesses

If you've made it through this entire book, you may be thinking "Wow! There's a lot to know about Web design!" That is true. While you've learned a lot, it isn't possible for any one book to teach you everything you might need to know to build a Web site and keep it running. I have read hundreds of books and other Web sites on the topic, and I still don't know everything that there is to know about Web design (though I like to think that I know a little). But I don't need to rely on what I know, because I know that I can always get help from other sources.

Determine your skills and weaknesses. The first thing to look at is what your skills are. But that can be hard. It's tempting to think that you're skilled at everything. But if you start thinking about your work habits, your skills might start coming into focus.

When you're trying to determine your weaknesses, don't be too hard on yourself. If this is the first Web site you've ever built,

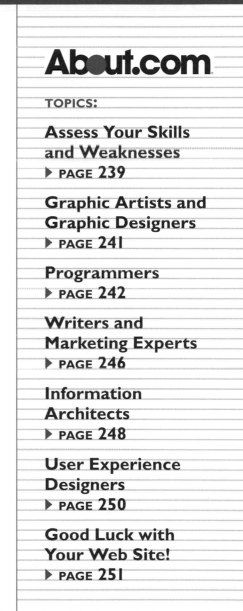

there are going to be things that you'll need to improve, but that's not a weakness. When you're trying to determine if you need to hire someone else to help you, you need to figure out what things you both don't like to work on and are not good at. If you enjoy working on something, you'll get better at it.

If you don't know what your skills and weaknesses are, ask yourself these questions:

- What is my favorite part of building a Web site?
- What tasks do I leave for last when building or maintaining my site?
- Which chapters in this book were the hardest for me to pay attention to?

If you're like most people, you enjoy doing those things that you're best at. That's the easiest way to tell where your skills lie. I like to program and code Web sites. I love thinking about how my site is going to work when it's all put together. That means that I'll end up with designs that are very spare (read "boring"). If I'm not working on the programming, I'm working on the content for my Web site. I don't particularly like taking photos or looking at pictures. Based on that, my skills are in programming and writing and my weaknesses are in graphics and design.

Then figure out where you need help. Once you have a sense of where your strengths and weaknesses are, you can start evaluating where you need help and where you just need to practice more.

There is always room for improvement, even in the things you excel at. Sometimes finding help is more about determining where you want help than where you need it. The thing about Web sites and Web design is that there is a lot of help available in many different forms.

ELSEWHERE ON THE WEB

▶ One of my favorite tools for analyzing just about anything is the SWOT analysis. This stands for strengths, weaknesses, opportunities, and threats. The About.com Entrepreneurs site has an excellent article on SWOT analysis (http://about.com/entrepreneurs/swot) that will help you learn how to use SWOT to evaluate and build your Web site and also how to determine what to do yourself and what to contract out.

Graphic Artists and Graphic Designers

There are many people out there who work on Web sites doing graphic design. According to the About.com Guides to Graphic Design, a graphic designer is someone who has an "understanding of type, color, and image and sound to create visual solutions to communications problems."

What do graphic designers do? A graphic designer can do a lot of things for a Web site. I have used graphic designers in the following capacities:

- **Web-site planning:** The designer created visual pictures of how the site would work that we used in pre-testing the site design with customers. In some cases, the images were simple, but they were better than words to get the point across.
- **Web-site layout design:** The designer created graphical mockups of how the page would look so that the HTML programmers (me and my team) could build the site.
- **Contextual design:** The designer provided ideas for the content of the Web site through visual cues that the writer wasn't aware of. Once the images were done, the writer had even more to write about for the site.
- **Graphics for the site:** This is the most common use of a Web graphic designer, where the designer is asked to create pictures to complement a site or an article or product.
- **Maintaining graphics:** A graphic designer may be asked to do anything from recreating the graphic in different languages to correcting problems that are found on the graphic after it's live. I've had graphic designers edit graphics with the wrong color in the background and graphics in which the company name was spelled wrong.

How do you find a good graphic artist? Before you hire a graphic artist to help you with your site, make sure you know what you're looking for. If you're hiring someone to build mock-ups for your design and layout, you'll want someone with different skills than someone who is going to be managing your Web-ready images for your Web site.

Keep in mind, as well, that most graphic designers are artists. They prefer to work on creative things rather than just fixing typos and correcting color issues. It's not uncommon for companies to hire a low-level graphic designer to do Web graphic maintenance. These designers don't usually create original images for the Web site. Rather, they take stock photography or even clip art and add text or manipulate them for the site. This is a perfectly reasonable use of a graphic designer, but if you don't have other, more creative jobs for them to do, you may be hiring and re-hiring for the position.

Since my skills are not suited to graphics, I like to have a graphical person available to work with on the Web sites I build. I typically will come up with the initial ideas and scope of the site with the client and then work with a designer to mock up several sample sites. With the mockups built, I usually don't need a graphic designer until I have pages that need actual graphics. For those I either use stock photography or hire someone to do the work I need. For the sites that I've maintained, I haven't needed a full-time graphic designer on staff, but for the corporate sites I've worked on, we've always had at least one and usually two or three designers on staff at all times.

Programmers

Programming on a Web site can mean many different things to different people. When I first started in Web development, I felt that HTML wasn't programming because it wasn't compiled. But

ELSEWHERE ON THE WEB

▶ Finding a designer can be challenging, but the About .com Graphic Design Guides have written a wonderful step-by-step tutorial to help you ask the right questions and get the designer you need (http://about.com/graphicdesign/hiredesigner). Mark Wright also gives some good advice on choosing a designer in his article "Find a Graphic Designer" (www.markwright.com/design.htm).

then I started writing Perl, and while Perl isn't compiled, it is still programming. And after a while I was doing many of the same things that I used to do with CGI scripts, only with HTML using additions like SSI and PHP or ColdFusion. So it started to feel like programming.

What do programmers do on Web sites? According to Dictionary.com, a program, when referring to computers, is "a sys tematic plan for the automatic solution of a problem by a computer" or "the precise sequence of instructions enabling a computer to solve a problem." The challenge of this definition is how you read it. If you focus on the word "automatic" and decide that that means "dynamic," then perhaps HTML doesn't meet the criteria. But when you look at the second definition, HTML does fit the definition because it is a precise set of instructions to allow a computer, through a Web browser, to solve a problem of how to display Web-page content.

Whether you agree that HTML is programming or not, there are lots of other languages that do fit the criteria of programming that you may not be ready to manage yourself on your Web site, such as these:

- CGI scripts for running form-to-e-mail scripts and other forms
- Advanced JavaScript such as Ajax for more interactive sites
- ASP, ColdFusion, JSP, or PHP connections with databases
- Flash applications and animations

Web programmers can be almost as diverse as the entire field of Web design. One of the things you'll find out very quickly is that while the skills of programming are convertible from one language to another (in other words, someone who knows C++ can learn

WHAT'S HOT

▶ Many people consider HTML to be a programming language when technically it's a markup language. In my poll asking if people consider HTML to be programming (http://about.com/webdesign/htmlpoll) nearly 50 percent of the people responding said that they consider it to be a programming language. This has sparked some heated debate in the comments of the poll.

to write Java), many programmers are not as flexible. In many cases an ASP programmer has never even looked at a PHP Web site and would never dream of writing one. I am somewhat guilty of this. I prefer the languages I know, such as Perl, PHP, and JSP.

Choose a good Web programmer. When you're trying to find a good Web programmer for your site, you need to know what you need on your site. You also need to know what your server can support. You can spend a lot of time interviewing and find the perfect programmer who is very knowledgeable in ASP, for example, but if your Web server does not support ASP, you'll both be frustrated. In one situation, the programmer spent his first three months on the job attempting to get us to change to a new system (from Perl to PHP). When it became obvious to him that we couldn't make that switch, he quit.

When you're trying to find a good Web programmer, think about the following aspects of the job you need done and the person you want to hire:

What is the job?
- Is it long term or short term?
- Will there be multiple programs to create?
- Do you expect your programmer to maintain the program(s) after they're built?

Many Web sites don't need a full-time Web programmer on staff. I worked for eight years at Symantec, and in that time, 80 percent of the programming that I did was form-to-e-mail scripts. I just modified my first script to meet the needs of the next form that was requested. If I'd hired a full-time Web programmer to do that, she would have been bored out of her mind after the first script was complete.

Instead, what works best is to hire someone as a contractor to build the script or program you need and then to teach you how to maintain it. Make sure you find someone who is willing to help you learn to maintain your script, or you'll be paying every time there is a minor hiccough on your Web server and the e-mail doesn't go through.

When considering hiring a contractor, you should think about the following:

What is the environment?

- Do you need a programmer on site?
- Does the programmer need to work standard hours?

It's easier to find contract programmers if you're willing to let them work the hours they are comfortable with. My experience is that many programmers are night owls and get most of their best work done after the rest of the world has gone to bed. If you need a program written fast, it's better to have it written when the programmer can do it rather than expecting them to come into an office and work from nine to five.

On the other hand, if you're looking for a programmer to join your team, make sure that she is ready to work the hours that you need her to be available. While she might work best from midnight to two, marketing team members are not usually awake then, and they will want to have a chance to talk to your programmer as well.

What do you want programmed?

- What language(s) does your server support?
- What language do you want your program written in?
- Does the programmer need to know HTML or other Web design programs?

TOOLS YOU NEED

▶ Finding the right contractor for a job can be difficult, but there are a lot of Web programmers who read the About.com Web Design/HTML Forum (http://about.com/webdesign/forums). If you post your request there, you'll get responses from lots of people with the skills you need to build scripts and other programs for your Web site. Another good place to post your jobs is on Web-development job banks (http://about.com/webdesign/jobbanks). These listings can help you understand what to expect from a programmer as well as how much it might cost.

This is the most important part of choosing a programmer. You need to know what you want built. Nothing is more frustrating to a contract programmer than a project where the first few weeks are spent the job. Most programmers charge primarily for the time they spend writing code, but if you haven't gotten your plans straight up front, you may be surprised at a bill that includes many hours of planning that you could have done on your own, without the programmer.

In Chapter 2, we discussed planning your Web site, and should have the start of a plan for the scripts and programs you would need on the site. You should know what programs your hosting service (Chapter 3) provides and whether or not you want to use them. All programming languages have pros and cons, and you should evaluate all of your options before you make a decision. Otherwise, the programmer you hire will decide for you. For one job I worked on, we completely switched our Windows Web servers over to Linux because a new programmer was persuasive enough to make that change.

Writers and Marketing Experts

You may not think you need a professional writer or marketer to work on your Web site, but you might be surprised. Writing is the primary mode of getting information across to your customers on Web pages, and hiring a professional to help you get the words right can make the difference between a good site and a great one.

What do Web writers do? You may be surprised to learn that Web writers are different from print writers in many ways. Remember, people read the Web differently than they do print. Think about this book you have in your hands. You may not have it in your hands at all; you may have it resting on a towel as you lounge on the beach. Or you may be lying in bed with the radio on in the background using it to help you fall asleep. (I hope not.) Or you may be sitting at your computer propping it open with a half-full, extra-foam macchiato as you try to follow along online.

Web pages are different. For one thing, if you spill your macchiato on a Web page, you'll never read another Web page with that computer again. You also can't read a Web page on the beach. Even if you have wireless and a sand-proof laptop, I can attest that the glare from the sun and water makes it almost impossible to see the screen. And falling asleep with a computer on your lap is not that comfortable.

When you hire a writer for your Web site, make sure that he knows how to write for the Web and that he understands the differences between writing for Web pages and writing for print publications. (If you need a reminder of the differences, review Chapter 6.)

Hiring a writer for a Web site is similar to hiring a writer of any sort. Look for writing skills and a portfolio that demonstrates that the person knows what she is doing when it comes to writing Web pages. If you are looking for content writers, focus on people who know your topic and have some credentials in the area. Don't make the mistake of assuming that you'll be able to hire people for copies or credit. Some Web sites don't pay for writing, but the majority pay at least a small amount for articles and information they use. Many paying sites don't put by-lines on the articles. If you're not willing to pay for Web content and you can't provide it yourself, you should reconsider the goals of your site.

Marketing is also important on Web pages. Many small companies don't want to spend anything in this area, either. If you don't have a lot of expertise in marketing or your company doesn't

WHAT'S HOT

▶ When you're looking for a Web writer, make sure that you see some portfolio samples from your prospective hires. Then, when you're looking over their work, make sure that you hire someone who follows standard Web-writing techniques. If your candidate uses links well, has a style that can be adapted to your site, and demonstrates an understanding of Web writing, you'll have a good hire.

have a marketing department, then having a marketing review of your Web site and materials would not be a bad idea.

When looking for a marketing consultant, keep in mind some of the following:

- **What is the person's experience?** You want someone who understands the needs of your Web site. If your site is product focused, look for a consultant who has done product marketing. If your site is content focused, look for a consultant who has experience with copy and content.
- **What media does the person focus on?** If you don't have a large budget, then hiring someone who does more television spots than radio or Internet ads is not a good idea.
- **Is the person willing to try new ideas?** A new firm might be more willing to try new things than an older, established company. But make sure that you check references.

Information Architects

Information architects and library scientists are a growing field in relation to Web design. In many ways, Web sites are like a giant warehouse of information. Information architects help you to categorize and organize that information so that both you and your customers can find it.

The challenge that many small-business Web sites face is that they don't think they need a library scientist or information architect for their site. It's easy to think that you'll be able to maintain the structure yourself, but before you try, ask yourself the following questions:

- Am I naturally organized?
- Is my organization system something that other people understand?

- Do I need a map of my file cabinet to find things?
- Is my family afraid to look for things in my filing system because they are afraid they'll never find their way out?
- Do any of the above questions about file cabinets apply to my files on my computer?

I honestly like to think of myself as naturally organized. I am organized in the sense that I like to pile things up. I know that in that pile on the right, about two thirds of the way down, is the bill from my credit card company (which I've paid), while on the left is the stack of things I need to read by Tuesday.

In my defense, I do find organizing information interesting. I like putting things into categories and giving them tags and being able to find them again later. Though I enjoy doing this, I still find that my Web sites become horribly muddled with conflicting terms and categories. Even on my site at About .com, I have this problem. What is the difference between my CSS Layout Templates category and my Web Site Templates category? When I first built them, I didn't really know. I didn't remember that I had the categories until I noticed that some of my free Web templates were in one category and some were in another.

An information architect helps you make sense of all that. She would tell you when to combine two categories and when to separate them out.

She also would help you find the right terms to use for naming your categories. For example, one of the most popular categories on my site is the "HTML and Web Design Tutorials" category. My editor wanted me to call it "Beginning HTML" or "Beginning Web Design" or a combination of the two. The problem with this title is that while it sounds good, it doesn't work for search-engine optimization; in other words, it's not what people are looking for on the Web. "Beginning HTML" is something that you might see at a bookstore or in a college catalog. But when people come to a Web site wanting to learn HTML, they tend to look for "HTML tutorials" because that's what they want.

User Experience Designers

A user experience designer looks at the Web site as a whole and incorporates solutions that move from the customers' needs out. The idea is that you need to create a site that is useful, usable, and findable for your customers so that they will find it more valuable and credible.

What do user experience (UX) designers do? UX designers are focused on more than the information architecture of a site. They look at all aspects of a Web site, from the design and layout of the interface to the interaction connections of the development side. I have worked with UX designers who focused primarily on the interface of the Web site, while others focused more on the interactivity elements. The best UX designers are those who understand that all Web sites are a combination of factors that interact to create the experience for the customer.

Finding a good UX designer is hard. This is not a job that has been around for years and years, and anyone who claims to have more than three to five years of experience as a UX designer is exaggerating at best. Chances are that they are claiming previous work as a Web designer or information architect as being under the umbrella of user experience.

In some ways, this claim is correct, as a good UX designer has skills in many Web-design and -development areas. When I'm looking for a good UX designer, I look for these things:

- Knowledge of Web sites and how to build Web applications
- An understanding of user testing and using the results

- The ability to set clear goals for Web sites
- Working knowledge of the coding tools required to build and maintain Web sites
- A good personality, as this person will have to work with all members of your team

If you're trying to decide if you need a UX designer, instead decide whether you need more assistance in multiple areas of your Web site. For example, if you need information-architecture assistance as well as content, a UX designer might be able to give you some of those things. In some ways, UX designers are like Web designers on steroids. They not only know how to build great-looking Web sites, they also know how to build Web sites that your customers will like and want to use.

Good Luck with Your Web Site!

Whether you build your site all by yourself or you hire outside people to help, you're embarking on an exciting new phase in your business. I hope that your site does well.

Remember that building a Web site is an ongoing process. One of the most exciting and frustrating aspects of Web design is that it's never finished. You can always work on your site more. Doing redesigns is just the start. You can add new products or articles, assess how your site is doing through customer surveys and reviews of your site statistics, and continually improve your search-engine optimization and speed of download. Plus, once you're comfortable in one technology, there are a huge number of other technologies that you can start learning.

Now that you've got a Web site up and running, get out there and start planning how you're going to improve it or how you're going to create your next Web site. This is the fun part!

Get Linked

The following Web sites will give you more information on getting outside help for building your Web site.

GRAPHICS

Understanding graphics is the first step toward understanding if you need a graphic designer. These links will help you get started with graphics and help you recognize if you need a professional.

http://about.com/webdesign/graphics

PROFESSIONAL WEB PROGRAMMER RESOURCES

A professional Web programmer can help you in lots of ways. These resources show various options and things you might want to hire someone to do for your site.

http://about.com/webdesign/proresources

Appendix A

HTML and CSS Library

HTML

The following elements are valid XHTML tags for use in Web documents. All these tags and more are listed in my online XHTML Tag Library (http://about.com/webdesign/htmltags).

A Tags–

`<a> . . . </a>`
The anchor tag is used to create links to other documents.

`<abbr> . . . </abbr>`
The abbreviation tag defines the enclosed text as an abbreviation.

`<acronym> . . . </acronym>`
The acronym tag defines the enclosed text as an acronym.

`<address> . . . </address>`
The address tag provides information about the authors of the Web page or site.

`<area />`
This tag defines the area of an image map that will be clickable and where clicking will go to.

B Tags–

`<b> . . . </b>`
The bold tag makes the enclosed text bold.

`<base />`
The base tag sets the base URI for relative paths within the document. It can also define the base target used in framesets.

`<bdo> . . . </bdo>`
The bidirectional text tag indicates the direction the enclosed text should be using.

`<big> . . . </big>`
This tag renders the enclosed text in a larger font.

`<blockquote> . . . </blockquote>`
The blockquote tag designates a long block of quoted text. It is usually used for long quotations where a paragraph break would be appropriate.

`<body>. . . </body>`
The body tag defines the contents of the Web page. If an element appears in this tag, it will show up on the Web page.

`<br />`
This tag forces a line break within the document.

`<button> . . . </button>`
This tag creates a versatile button for HTML forms.

C Tags–

`<!-- . . . --> HTML Comment`
Text enclosed in these codes will not appear on the Web page, but will show up as comments within the HTML code.

`<caption> . . . </caption>`
This tag is for captions, which describe HTML tables and their contents.

`<cite> . . . </cite>`
Use the cite tag to indicate a citation or reference a source.

`<code> . . . </code>`
Text inside the code tag is computer code.

```
<col />
```
This tag defines the columns and their appearance in Web tables.

```
<colgroup> . . . </colgroup>
```
This tag defines groups of columns within an HTML table.

D Tags–

```
<!DOCTYPE>
```
Not an XHTML tag, but an XML tag that defines which document-type definition the Web page will be using.

```
<dd> . . . </dd>
```
The dd tag defines a term in a definition list.

```
<del> . . . </del>
```
This tag indicates text that has been deleted from a previous version of the document.

```
<dfn> . . . </dfn>
```
Use this tag to define a term the first time it's used in a Web document.

```
<div> . . . </div>
```
This tag defines logical divisions within the Web document.

```
<dl> . . . </dl>
```
The dl tag indicates that the enclosed elements are a definition list.

```
<dt> . . . </dt>
```
Text enclosed in this tag is the term portion of a definition list.

E Tags–

```
<em> . . . </em>
```
The enclosed text should be displayed with some emphasis (usually italics).

F Tags–

```
<fieldset> . . . </fieldset>
```
Fieldsets are used in HTML forms to group form fields and labels that are thematically related.

```
<form> . . . </form>
```
Use the form tag to create HTML forms on your Web pages.

```
<frame> . . . </frame>
```
Use the frame tag to create a frame within a frameset.

```
<frameset> . . . </frameset>
```
A frameset is a container tag for a framed Web page.

G Tags–

There are no XHTML elements that start with G.

H Tags–

```
<h1>. . .</h1>, <h2>. . .</h2>, <h3>. .
.</h3>, <h4>. . .</h4>, <h5>. . .</h5>,
<h6>. . .</h6>
```
These elements define logical headings within an HTML document. H1 is the most important and H6 is the least.

```
<head> . . . </head>
```
The head tag encloses information about the document, including meta data, styles, and associated scripts.

```
<hr />
```
This tag creates a horizontal line in the document.

```
<html> . . . </html>
```
This is the container element for every XHTML document.

I Tags–

```
<i> . . . </i>
```
This tag converts the enclosed text to italics.

```
<iframe> . . . </iframe>
```
This tag creates an inline frame in the document.

```
<img />
```
This tag adds an image to the document.

```
<input />
```
This tag creates an input field for an HTML form.

```
<ins> . . . </ins>
```
This tag denotes that the enclosed text has been inserted into an edited document.

J Tags–

There are no XHTML elements that start with J.

K Tags–

```
<kbd> . . . </kbd>
```
This tag defines the enclosed text as text that should be entered by the user, as with a keyboard.

L Tags–

```
<label> . . . </label>
```
This tag assigns an informative label to a form field or control.

```
<legend> . . . </legend>
```
This tag assigns a caption to HTML form fieldsets.

```
<li> . . . </li>
```
This tag defines the enclosed content as a list item.

```
<link />
```
This tag links the current document to related documents and style sheets.

M Tags–

```
<map> . . . </map>
```
This tag defines a client-side image map.

```
<meta />
```
This tag provides additional information about the document.

N Tags–

```
<noframes> . . . </noframes>
```
This tag defines the content that should be displayed to user-agents that don't recognize HTML frames.

```
<noscript> . . . </noscript>
```
This tag defines the content that should be displayed to user-agents that don't render scripts.

O Tags–

```
<object> . . . </object>
```
This tag is used to insert non-standard elements into the document like applets or video.

```
<ol> . . . </ol>
```
This tag defines an ordered or numbered list.

```
<optgroup> . . . </optgroup>
```
This tag defines a group of options in a select list.

```
<option> . . . </option>
```
This tag defines an element in a select or drop-down list.

P Tags–

```
<p> . . . </p>
```
This tag defines the enclosed content as a paragraph.

```
<param />
```
The parameter tag indicates a value that should be used by an object.

```
<pre> . . . </pre>
```
This tag defines the enclosed content as pre-formatted text.

Q Tags–

```
<q> . . . </q>
```
This tag defines short quotations.

R Tags–

There are no XHTML elements that start with R.

S Tags–

```
<samp> . . . </samp>
```
This tag defines the enclosed content as sample output from a script or program.

```
<script> . . . </script>
```
This tag inserts a script into the document.

`<select> . . . </select>`
This tag creates a select or drop-down list in an HTML form.

`<small> . . . </small>`
This tag renders the enclosed text smaller than the base font size.

`<span> . . . </span>`
This tag provides for inline formatting of the enclosed content.

`<strong> . . . </strong>`
This tag indicates that the enclosed content should be displayed with strong emphasis (usually bold).

`<style> . . . </style>`
This tag places style properties on the page.

`<sub> . . . </sub>`
This tag defines the enclosed content as a subscript.

`<sup> . . . </sup>`
This tag defines the enclosed content as a super-script.

T Tags–

`<table> . . . </table>`
This tag defines an HTML table.

`<tbody> . . . </tbody>`
This tag defines the body rows of an HTML table.

`<td> . . . </td>`
This tag defines table cells in an HTML table.

`<textarea> . . . </textarea>`
This tag defines a large, multi-line text entry box in an HTML form.

`<tfoot> . . . </tfoot>`
This tag defines the footer rows in an HTML table.

`<th> . . . </th>`
This tag defines header cells in an HTML table.

`<thead> . . . </thead>`
This tag defines the header rows in an HTML table.

`<title> . . . </title>`
This tag defines the title of the document.

`<tr> . . . </tr>`
This tag defines a row in an HTML table.

`<tt> . . . </tt>`
This tag defines the enclosed content as mono-spaced or teletype.

U Tags–

`<ul> . . . </ul>`
This tag defines an unordered or bulleted list.

V Tags–

`<var> . . . </var>`
This tag defines the enclosed content as a variable.

W,X,Y,Z Tags–

There are no XHTML elements that start with W.

There are no XHTML elements that start with X.

There are no XHTML elements that start with Y.

There are no XHTML elements that start with Z.

CSS Style Properties

Once you have your HTML written, you'll want to style it with these CSS style properties. This lists both CSS 1 and CSS 2 properties. All these properties and more are listed in the CSS Style Properties Library online (http://about.com/web design/cssstylelibrary).

A Properties–

`:active`
The active pseudo-class. Matches on links as they are being clicked on.

:after

The :after pseudo-element. Defines generated content to be placed after the element.

azimuth

Defines the location of the sound when the element is read.

B Properties–

:before

Before pseudo-element. Defines generated content to be placed before the element.

background

Defines all aspects of the element's background.

background-attachment

Defines if the background is attached to the canvas or if it scrolls with content.

background-color

Defines the color of the background.

background-image

Defines the image used in the background.

background-position

Defines the location (x,y) of the background image.

background-repeat

Defines whether the background image should tile and how it should tile.

border

Defines the border properties of the element.

border-bottom

Defines the bottom border properties of the element.

border-bottom-color

Defines the color of the bottom border.

border-bottom-style

Defines the style of the bottom border.

border-bottom-width

Defines the width of the bottom border.

border-collapse

Defines which of two methods should be used to display HTML table borders.

border-color

Defines the color of the border.

border-left

Defines the properties of the left border of the element.

border-left-color

Defines the color of the left border.

border-left-style

Defines the style of the left border.

border-left-width

Defines the width of the left border.

border-right

Defines the properties of the right border.

border-right-color

Defines the color of the right border.

border-right-style

Defines the style of the right border.

border-right-width

Defines the width of the right border.

border-spacing

Defines the distance that separates adjoining table cell borders.

border-style

Defines the style of the border of the element.

border-top

Defines the properties of the top border.

border-top-color

Defines the color of the top border.

border-top-style

Defines the style of the top border.

border-top-width

Defines the width of the top border.

border-width

Defines the width of the border of the element.

bottom

Defines how far the bottom of the element is offset from the bottom of the containing element.

C Properties–

caption-side

Defines where the table caption will display.

clear

Defines the sides of the element that should not float.

clip

Defines the portion of the element's content that is visible.

color

Defines the foreground color of the element.

content

Defines the generated content to be used with :before and :after pseudo-elements.

counter-increment

Defines the names of counters and how much they are incremented.

counter-reset

Defines what the counters should be reset to.

cue

Defines an auditory icon played to distinguish and delimit the element.

cue-after

Defines the auditory icon to be played after the element.

cue-after

Defines the auditory icon to be played before the element.

cursor

Defines the type of cursor to be displayed.

D Properties–

direction

Defines the direction the text will display.

display

Defines the way the element should display in the window.

E Properties–

elevation

Defines the height of the sound when the element is read.

empty-cells

Defines how borders and backgrounds will render around table cells with no content.

F Properties–

:first-child

The first-child pseudo-class. Matches on an element that is the first child of the parent element.

:first-letter

First letter pseudo-element. Defines styles for the first letter of an element.

:first-line

First line pseudo-element. Defines styles for the first line of an element.

float

Defines the side around which other elements will flow.

:focus

Focus pseudo-class. Matches elements while they have the focus.

font

Shorthand property to define the font style, variant, weight, size, line-height, and family.

font-family

Defines the font family.

font-size

Defines the font size.

font-style

Defines the style of the font.

font-variant
Defines whether the font is normal or small-caps.

font-weight
Defines how light or dark the font should display.

G Properties–

There are no CSS properties that start with G.

H Properties–

height
Defines the height of the element.

:hover
Hover pseudo-class. Matches elements as you put your mouse over them.

I Properties–

There are no CSS properties that start with I.

J Properties–

There are no CSS properties that start with J.

K Properties–

There are no CSS properties that start with K.

L Properties–

:lang
Language pseudo-class. Matches on the language defined in the document.

left
Defines how far the left side of the element will be offset from the container element.

letter-spacing
Defines the amount of space between letters.

line-height
Defines the height of each line.

:link
Link pseudo-class. Matches unvisited links.

list-style
A shorthand property to define the list type, position, and image.

list-style-image
Defines the image used in a list.

list-style-position
Defines the placement of the bullet or number in a list.

list-style-type
Defines the type of bullet or number in a list.

M Properties–

margin
A shorthand property defining the margin top, right, bottom, and left.

margin-bottom
Defines the bottom margin of the element.

margin-left
Defines the left margin of the element.

margin-right
Defines the right margin of the element.

margin-top
Defines the top margin of the element.

max-height
Defines the largest height the element should have.

max-width
Defines the largest width the element should have.

min-height
Defines the smallest height the element should have.

min-width
Defines the smallest width the element should have.

N Properties–

There are no CSS properties that start with N.

O Properties–

orphans
Defines the minimum number of lines that should be left at the bottom of a page.

outline
A shorthand property defining the outline color, style, and width.

outline-color
Defines the color of the outline.

outline-style
Defines the style of the outline.

outline-width
Defines the width of the outline.

overflow
Defines what should happen to excess content when it exceeds the defined size of the element.

P Properties–

padding
A shorthand property that defines the padding top, right, bottom, and left.

padding-bottom
Defines the bottom padding of the element.

padding-left
Defines the left padding of the element.

padding-right
Defines the right padding of the element.

padding-top
Defines the top padding of the element.

page-break-after
Defines where forced page breaks should appear.

page-break-before
Defines where forced page breaks should appear.

page-break-inside
Defines whether a page break should appear when inside an element.

pause-after
Defines a pause observed after speaking the element's content.

pause-before
Defines a pause observed before speaking the element's content.

pause
A shorthand property defining the pause before and after speaking the element's content.

pitch
Defines the average pitch of the speaking voice when the element is read.

pitch-range
Defines the variation in pitch when the element is read.

play-during
Defines a sound to play in the background while the element is read.

position
Defines how the element will be positioned.

Q Properties–

quotes
Defines the quotation marks for embedded quotations.

R Properties–

richness
Defines the richness or brightness of the speaking voice when the element is read.

right
Defines how far the right side of the element is off-set from the container.

S Properties–

speak
Defines whether the text should be rendered audibly and how.

speak-header
Defines when the table headers should be spoken aloud.

speak-numeral
Defines how numerals are spoken.

speak-punctuation
Defines how punctuation should be spoken.

speech-rate
Defines the speed at which the element is read.

stress
Defines the height of local peaks in intonation when the element is read.

T Properties–

table-layout
Defines the algorithm used to lay out tables.

text-align
Defines the horizontal alignment of content in the element.

text-decoration
Defines effects on text such as underline, overline, line-through, no underline, and blink.

text-indent
Defines the indentation of the first line of the element.

text-shadow
Defines a shadow around or beside the text.

text-transform
Defines the case of the element's text.

U Properties–

Unicode-bidi
Defines whether or not the direction of the text can be changed.

V Properties–

vertical-align
Defines the alignment of the element vertically on the line.

visibility
Defines whether or not the element boxes are displayed.

:visited
Visited pseudo-class. Matches on visited links.

voice-family
Defines a list of voice family names to use when the content is read aloud.

volume
Defines the median volume of the spoken element.

top
Defines how far the top of the element is offset from the container.

W Properties–

widows
Defines the minimum number of lines that must be left at the top of a page.

white-space
Defines how white space within the element is treated.

width
Defines the width of the element.

word-spacing
Defines the amount of space between words.

X Properties–

There are no CSS properties that start with X.

Y Properties–

There are no CSS properties that start with Y.

Z Properties–

z-index
Defines the stack level of the box in the current context and whether there is a local stacking context.

Appendix B

Glossary

A/B testing

A/B testing is a process of testing two designs at the same time to determine which has a better impact on the goals of the test.

Accessibility

Accessibility is the degree to which a Web page is usable by people with disabilities.

Ajax

Ajax is a scripting technique that uses asynchronous JavaScript and a server-side scripting language like Perl to generate Web pages that update inside the browser window rather than requiring a complete page refresh. This makes the Web pages feel more like desktop applications.

Applet

An applet is a Java application that runs inside a Web page.

ASP

ASP stands for active server pages. It is a programming language for Web developers to create dynamic, database-driven Web pages. It usually is found on Windows servers.

Attribute

An attribute is information included in an HTML element that provides more information about that element. For example, the <img /> element requires the source attribute to display an image <img src="image location" />.

Bandwidth

Bandwidth is the amount of information that can be passed over a network connection in a period of time. Bandwidth is usually measured in bits per second (bps) or kilobits per second (kbps).

Blog

A blog (shortened form of Weblog) is a Web page that has short frequent updates put up in a reverse chronological order (most recent first).

Blogging tool

A blogging tool is a piece of software that allows you to write a Weblog. Some examples are Blogger, TypePad, and WordPress.

Breadcrumb trail

A breadcrumb trail on a Web page is a form of hierarchical navigation that shows the user the route that was taken through the Web site to get to that page.

Cascading style sheets

Cascading style sheets, or CSS, is a language on the Web that is used to define the look and feel of Web pages and Web documents.

CGI

CGI stands for common gateway interface. CGI are scripts and programs that run on the server to add dynamic interactions on Web pages.

Clip art

Clip art is a collection of images, usually graphics rather than photographs, that can be used in various documents. While some clip art is free or free for non-commercial use, it is not all free. Do not assume that because something is labeled clip art it is free for any use.

CMS

See Content management system.

Colocation

Colocation is the purchase of space in the data center of another company to host your Web-server hardware. When you buy colocation, you can buy the space on the rack and access to the Internet backbone or fully managed systems.

Content management system

A content management system (CMS) is a system to control and manage content on Web pages.

CSS

See Cascading style sheets.

Doctype

The doctype indicates the HTML version used in the current document.

Document object model

The document object model, or DOM, is the protocol that binds together JavaScript and the HTML in the Web pages.

DOM

See Document object model.

DSL

DSL, for digital subscriber line, is a high-speed Internet connection.

Element

An element in Web design and HTML is the basic building block of an HTML document. An element can have an opening and closing tag, such as the <a></a> anchor element or be a singleton element with only one tag, such as the <img /> image tag.

Entry page

An entry page is any page on your Web site where people arrive first.

Flash

Flash is a dynamic application that runs inside of Web pages. It uses vector graphics to create animations and forms.

Font

A font is a collection of glyphs into a typeface. In CSS, the font property controls the font family, font size, and font weight.

FTP

FTP stands for file transfer protocol. It is the way you transfer files from your local computer to a Web server and back.

Full path

A full path is a complete path to a document on any server. A full path can reference documents on the same server by starting at the first slash after the domain name, or it can reference documents on other servers by including the domain name as well as the path to the resource.

GIF

GIF stands for graphics interchange format. A GIF is a graphics format suitable for flat-color images.

Hosting service provider

A hosting service provider provides space on a Web server for people to put up Web pages.

htaccess

Usually called .htaccess, htaccess refers to a method of securing directories and access on Apache Web servers.

HTML

HTML stands for HyperText Markup Language. This is the language that Web pages are written in.

HTML editor

An HTML editor is a software tool to edit Web pages. It can come in both WYSIWYG and text editor versions.

Internationalization

Internationalization is the process where a Web page or other document is localized from one language and culture to another. It is abbreviated as i18n.

Internet service provider

An Internet service provider (or ISP) is a company that sells access to the Internet to companies and individuals.

JPEG

JPEG stands for joint photographic experts group. A JPEG is a graphics format best suited for photographs. It is also spelled JPG.

Mailto link

A mailto link is an anchor on a Web page that opens an e-mail client to send an e-mail message.

Operating system

The operating system is the software that makes the computer run.

Orphan

An orphan is a page that is not linked to from anywhere on the Web site.

OS

OS stands for operating system. It is the software that makes the computer run.

PHP

PHP stands for hypertext pre-processor. It is a programming language for Web developers to create dynamic, database-driven Web pages.

Pixel

A pixel is a single dot on a computer screen. Images on computers are made up of tiny square dots or pixels.

PNG

PNG stands for portable network graphics. It is a graphics format similar to GIF that is best suited to flat color images.

Podcast

A podcast is a method of publishing audio files to the Internet so that they can be downloaded and listened to using an MP3 player.

Property

A CSS property is a command in CSS that defines how an element should be styled.

Referrer

The referrer on a Web page is the Web site that the customer came from before coming to the current page.

Relative path

A relative path is a partial path to a document on the same server as the referencing document. The path is defined as relative to the referencing document.

Rich text

Rich text is ASCII text with formatting included. This means that the font family, bold or italics, and font size are all included in rich text and are not included in ASCII text.

Roll-over

A roll-over is when an image changes when the mouse moves over it. Roll-over images and text are added to Web pages to make them more interactive.

Selector

A CSS selector is the element that the CSS style will be applied to.

SEO

SEO stands for search-engine optimization. SEO is the process of optimizing Web pages so that they will appear higher in search engines.

Server

A Web server is a computer that hosts Web pages. It is connected to the Internet and has a Web-server program, like Apache or iPlanet, running on it to display the Web pages.

SSH

SSH is a secure shell protocol to allow you to connect to a remote computer system in a secure fashion. It provides similar access as telnet sessions, but over an encrypted connection.

SSL

SSL stands for secure socket layer. It is an Internet protocol used to encrypt data transmissions over the Web. Web pages that use SSL have a URL that starts with `https://` rather than `http://`.

Stock photography

Stock photographs are photos that are sold to be used and reused for commercial design purposes. They are usually of common landmarks, ideas, or events that can be reused in various applications.

Tag

A tag in HTML is a grouping of characters surrounded by < and > characters that indicate the start and end of an HTML element. The `<a>` tag is the start of a link element and the `</a>` tag is the end of a link element.

Telnet

Telnet is a standard protocol for accessing remote computer systems. Also referred to as shell access.

Text editor

An HTML text editor is a software tool that edits Web pages directly in the HTML.

T1

A T1 line is a very high-speed Internet connection (1.544Mbits per second).

URL

URL stands for uniform resource locator. It is the address of a document or other resource on the Internet. Web URLs typically look like this: `http://webdesign.about.com/index.htm`.

Web hosting

A Web hosting provider provides space on a Web server for people to put up Web pages. The term Web hosting refers to the use of that space on the Web server.

Web site

A Web site is a grouping of Web pages accessed on the Internet through a Web browser like Internet Explorer or Firefox.

Weblog

See Blog.

WYSIWYG

Pronounced like whizzy-wig, this stands for "what you see is what you get." It is a type of HTML editor that allows you to edit your Web pages in a visual mode, rather than relying on the HTML code alone.

XHTML

XHTML stands for eXtensible HyperText Markup Language. It is a version of HTML 4.01 rewritten to be valid XML.

XML

XML stands for eXtensible Markup Language. It is a markup language built to define the structure and semantics of other markup languages.

Appendix C

Other Sites and Further Reading

Other Sites

Chapter 1: The Big Picture

FTP Voyager

www.ftpvoyager.com

This is my favorite FTP client. I use it all the time.

Dreamweaver

www.adobe.com/products/dreamweaver

Dreamweaver is one of the best HTML editors available for professional Web designers.

HomeSite

www.adobe.com/products/homesite

HomeSite is my HTML editor of choice. It is a text editor that is very easy to use.

BBEdit

www.barebones.com/products/bbedit

BBEdit is one of the most popular Web editors for the Macintosh.

nVu

www.nvu.com

If you don't want to pay anything for your Web editor, then check out nVu. It's easily the best free HTML editor I've ever seen.

PuTTY

www.chiark.greenend.org.uk/~sgtatham/putty

PuTTY is a free SSH client.

Photoshop

www.adobe.com/products/photoshop

Adobe's Photoshop is my favorite graphics editor.

XML Spy

www.altova.com/products/xmlspy/xml_editor. html

XML Spy is a great program for editing XML documents.

Chapter 2: Building a Site Structure

Planning Your Web Site

http://skdesigns.com/faq/plan

SKDesigns builds Web pages, and this document explains what they will help you do. It's a great start for thinking about how to plan your Web site.

Planning Your Web-Site Design from Adobe

www.adobe.com/support/dreamweaver/layout/site_planning

Learn how to create goals for your Web site and structure it in the planning stages.

Planning a Usable Web Site

www.webcredible.co.uk/user-friendly-resources/web-usability/plan-usable-website. shtml

This site presents three steps to a usable Web site.

Chapter 3: Hosting Your Web Site

Host Analyst

www.webhostinganalyst.com

This is a great research site to help you find the Web host that's right for you.

The Free Web Hosting Decision

http://personalweb.about.com/cs/homepage-hosting/a/402hosting.htm

Trying to decide what hosting provider to use is hard enough, but add to that the cost and it can be crazy. The About.com Guide to Personal Web Pages has an article that helps you decide whether to use free hosting or not.

Chapter 4: All about Code

W3Schools

www.w3schools.com

This site offers a lot of resources and information on building Web pages.

Chapter 5: Creating a Content or Article Page

A List Apart: Writing

http://alistapart.com/topics/content/writing

A List Apart is one of the premier Web magazines about building Web pages, and this section on writing covers all you need to know about creating great Web content.

Writing for the Web

www.useit.com/papers/webwriting

Jakob Nielsen offers a lot of articles and information on how to write for the Web.

Chapter 6: Creating a Product Page

Café Press

www.cafepress.com

Café Press is a great way to get your products online because they help you create the products.

Chapter 7: Contact Us and Information Pages

E-mail

http://email.about.com

The About.com Email Guide has the most information about staying in contact on the Internet that you'll ever find.

Chapter 8: Navigating Your Site

Listamatic

http://css.maxdesign.com.au/listamatic

There are hundreds of lists that use CSS and simple HTML to get vastly different designs.

Chapter 9: Building Your Home Page

Joe Burns' Thoughts on Building a Home Page

www.htmlgoodies.com/beyond/reference/article.php/3472871

Joe Burns has only four basic rules for building a home page. But if you follow them, your home page will be so much better.

How to Convince Clients They Don't Need a Splash Page

www.dci.in/portfolio/web_design_splash.asp

This article looks at some of the common justifications for splash pages and debunks them.

Chapter 10: Search Engine Optimization (SEO) and Site Promotion

Search Engine Watch

http://searchenginewatch.com

If you're interested in learning more about SEO, then Search Engine Watch is where to start. This site has everything about search engines you could ever hope to know.

Chapter 11: Making Money with Advertising and E-commerce

E-commerce Solutions

http://onlinebusiness.about.com/od/shopping-carts

If you're wondering how you can make money with e-commerce, start with the About.com Guide to Online Business.

E-commerce Times

www.ecommercetimes.com

This site provides lots of articles and information about growing your business online.

Chapter 12: Optimizing Your Site for Speed

Web Site Optimization

www.websiteoptimization.com

This is the companion site to the book *Speed Up Your Site*. There are hundreds of ideas and suggestions for how to improve your site download speeds, and the tools are helpful for analyzing your pages.

Chapter 13: Making Your Site Accessible

Web Accessibility Initiative (WAI)

www.w3.org/WAI

This is where to go to get the most up-to-date thoughts and information about Web accessibility.

WebAIM

www.webaim.org

Here you'll find more articles and information at a less technical level about Web accessibility.

Chapter 14: Adding Drama: Flash, DHTML, Ajax, and More

Flash

www.adobe.com/products/flash/flashpro

If you want to build Flash applications and Web sites, then your best tool is Flash itself.

Ajax: A New Approach to Web Applications

www.adaptivepath.com/publications/essays/archives/000385.php

This is the article that started the Ajax revolution.

Chapter 15: When to Hire Help

Web Design Plaza

www.webdesignplaza.com

This great search engine lets you fill in the details of what type of help you need and then matches you to designers.

Further Reading

Getting started on your Web site can be challenging. Planning a site, developing the strategy, and finding tools to use are all part of the process. These books and resources will help you start building your site.

Cascading Style Sheets The Designers Edge, by Molly Holzschlag

Molly will take you through CSS gently but with an eye toward creating great design.

Designing Web Audio, by Josh Beggs and Dylan Thede

> Audio on the Web is as tricky as building graphics or flash, but most people don't know much about how to do it. This book will help you create great sound files that don't take forever to download.

Designing Web Sites That Sell, by Shayne Bowman and Chris Willis

> There are a lot of books available that will teach you HTML, but this book will help you make better e-commerce Web sites.

Don't Make Me Think, by Steve Krug

> Usability made easy, that's what this book does. The secret is to make sure your customers never have to think while they're on your site.

The Elements of User Experience, by Jesse James Garrett

> If you are looking to learn more about user experience as it relates primarily to Web sites, you can't go wrong with this book. You'll learn the basics of Web design from a user-centered focus.

Head Rush Ajax, by Brett McLaughlin

> I loved reading this book almost more than I loved writing the Ajax it taught me.

HTML: The Definitive Guide, by Bill Kennedy and Chuck Musciano

> This is the only book you'll ever need for writing HTML.

Learning Web Design, by Jennifer Niederst

> If you want to learn Web design, you won't go wrong in picking up this book.

Publish and Prosper: Blogging for Your Business, by D. L. Byron

> This book will take you through all the steps you need to get your business blogging and how to profit from it.

Speed Up Your Site: Web-Site Optimization, by Andrew B. King

> Optimizing your Web site is all about speed and download times. If you have a well-optimized site, you'll have a site that downloads quickly, even on slower connections.

Web Navigation: Designing the User Experience, by Jennifer Flemming

> If you need help building Web navigation, this book should be your first stop.

Web-Site Measurement Hacks, by Eric T. Peterson

> This is a great introduction to Web analytics.

The Zen of CSS Design, by Dave Shae and Molly Holzschlag

> If you have some CSS experience, this book will help you make it even better by seeing what is possible with CSS design.

Index

D

Databases, sites with, 234–35
Delphi, 237
DHTML, 220–26, 230–31
Directories, 26–27
Division tags, 60–61
Domain names, 40–43,
   42–43
Donations, 75, 182–83

E

E-commerce, **100**, 169–70.
   See also Money, making
E-mail addresses, 108–10
Employment pages, 107
Error pages, 121–22, 126–28

F

Flash, 9, 28, 164, 190, 191,
   226–27, 230, 231–32, 233
FTP, 8, 37–38

G

Getting started, 1–2, 12–13.
   See also HTML editor
   features and options
Global pages, 5–6, 210–13
Glossary, 265–68

Goals for site, 9–12, 15–17.
   See also specific page types
Graphic artists/designers,
   241–42, **253**
Graphics editors, 7–8

H

Hiding text, 162–63
Hierarchy of technology, 46–
   47, 229–30
Hiring help, 239–**53**
   assessing your skills/
      weaknesses and needs,
      239–40
   graphic artists/designers,
      241–42, **253**
   information architects,
      248–50
   marketing, 247–48
   programmers, 242–46, 253
   user experience (UX)
      designers, 250–51
   writers, 246–47
Home pages, 135–**52**
   customers not seeing,
      137–38
   deciding what to include,
      139–42
   defined, 20
   goals of, 24–25, 138–39

   importance of, 135–36,
      137–38
   information-centered,
      144–47
   layout options, 143–51
   load time, 142–43, 186. *See*
      also Speed, optimizing
   navigation, 148–51
   requirements, 136–37
   splash pages, 143–44
Hosting, 31–**44**
   choosing provider, 32–40,
      44
   colocation, **44**
   importance of, 31–32
   inexpensive and free,
      42–43
   provider types, 39–40
   space for pages, 35–36
   tools, 37–39
   virtual and physical access
      to, 34
HTML, 45–46, 47–61
   about, 47–49, **66**
   division tags, 60–61
   forms, 111–15, **118**
   image tags, 56–58
   link tags, 58–60
   list tags, 54–56
   minimizing, for speed,
      192–97

About.com

INFORMATION DELIVERED IN A REVOLUTIONARY NEW WAY.

The Internet. Books. Experts. This is how—and where—we get our information today. And now, the best of these resources are available together in a revolutionary new series of how-to guides from **About.com** and Adams Media.

The About.com Guide to Acoustic Guitar
ISBN 10: 1-59869-098-1
ISBN 13: 978-1-59869-098-9

The About.com Guide to Baby Care
ISBN 10: 1-59869-274-7
ISBN 13: 978-1-59869-274-7

The About.com Guide to Family Crafts
ISBN 10: 1-59869-346-8
ISBN 13: 978-1-59869-346-1

The About.com Guide to Getting in Shape
ISBN 10: 1-59869-278-X
ISBN 13: 978-1-59869-278-5

The About.com Guide to Having a Baby
ISBN 10: 1-59869-095-7
ISBN 13: 978-1-59869-095-8

The About.com Guide to Home Cooking
ISBN 10: 1-59869-396-4
ISBN 13: 978-1-59869-396-6

The About.com Guide to Home Decorating
ISBN 10: 1-59869-347-6
ISBN 13: 978-1-59869-347-8

The About.com Guide to Job Searching
ISBN 10: 1-59869-097-3
ISBN 13: 978-1-59869-097-2

The About.com Guide to Online Research
ISBN 10: 1-59869-503-2
ISBN 13: 978-1-59869-503-8

The About.com Guide to Owning a Dog
ISBN 10: 1-59869-279-8
ISBN 13: 978-1-59869-279-2

The About.com Guide to Quilting
ISBN 10: 1-59869-344-1
ISBN 13: 978-1-59869-344-2

The About.com Guide to Shortcut Cooking
ISBN 10: 1-59869-273-9
ISBN 13: 978-1-59869-273-0

The About.com Guide to Southern Cooking
ISBN 10: 1-59869-096-5
ISBN 13: 978-1-59869-096-5

The About.com Guide to Web Design
ISBN 10: 1-59869-378-6
ISBN 13: 978-1-59869-378-2

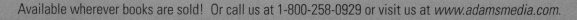

Available wherever books are sold! Or call us at 1-800-258-0929 or visit us at *www.adamsmedia.com*.